Praise for *I Can [*

"Anna Madsen has a unique, prophetic voice as a Lutheran theologian. With passion and erudition, she brings Martin Luther's liberating discovery of grace as a charge for Christian communities today to make justice happen, with hope embodied. 'Our God is revealed in every move we make, and people are watching.'"
Kirsi Stjerna, Pacific Lutheran Theological Seminary

"Madsen has gifted us with a systematic response to this divided, tragic, beautiful world, to her own personal tragedy and how it affected everything, and to the call that Christians desperately need to hear right now to truly practice 'justice and peace in all the earth.'"
Beth Birkholz, pastor at Holy Cross Lutheran Church, Livonia, Michigan

"In the words of Habakkuk 2:2, *write it down, make it clear, and run with it.* That is exactly what Anna Madsen has done in this book, connecting dots across time and space to help individuals and the church continue to reform. The church today is not our grandparents' Lutheran church. It is called to address the current issues facing the least of these, through the gospel of Jesus Christ."
William C. Hamilton Jr., copastor of St. John's Lutheran Church, Jacksonville, Florida

"Anna Madsen's work is an unfolding wonder to me. Her deeply spiritual reflections on very real issues in life and society hit me sometimes like a prophetic slap. And yet, beneath the critique and the concern for real human sin, the whisper of God's mercy and love can always be heard. I am grateful for all I have learned—and continue to learn—from her."
Guy Erwin, bishop of the Southwest California Synod, ELCA

"Anna Madsen was able to take 'what we've heard and learned' from Sunday school, Catechism, sermons, conversations, and Bible studies and expound her theological thoughts in a way that will cause readers to pause and reflect on a wider view of possibilities. Readers are sure to get a broader sense of their own faith and practices as they stretch their concept of God. Our challenge as disciples is not to accept the status quo but to put our faith into action—action in everyday life. I was moved by the concept of the anticipatory church and pray that it is lifted by others as well as a vision of God's possibilities."

Victoria Hamilton, copastor of St. John's Lutheran Church, Jacksonville, Florida

I Can Do No Other

I Can Do No Other

The Church's New
Here We Stand Moment

Anna M. Madsen

Fortress Press

Minneapolis

I CAN DO NO OTHER
The Church's New Here We Stand Moment

Cover image: iStock © 2019; Easter. Crucifixion. Three crosses in shadows on grunge background by FSTOP123
Cover design: Alisha Lofgren
Typesetting: PerfecType, Nashville, TN

Print ISBN: 978-1-5064-2737-9
eBook ISBN: 978-1-5064-3823-8

To my late mama, Marge, shalom live-er;
my father, George, shalom preacher; and my children,
Karl and Else, shalom bestowers

CONTENTS

PREFACE

In 2004, an accident that killed my husband gave my son a traumatic brain injury. My boy was only on the cusp of three, and my baby girl had been but just eight months in my arms. The year before, I had received my PhD, earned for a dissertation on the presence of God in the midst of suffering. And then, suddenly, I wasn't studying suffering; I was living it.

Everything changed: my family constellation, my vocational trajectory, and, not least of all, my understanding of the very theology in which I had just been deemed an Official Expert.

Academically, I had understood that God stirs when nothing but despair does. But I didn't know the existential essence of that theological claim in the way that a saturated soul knows a truth, knows a love, knows a loss.

Compounding the trauma of the accident was the trauma of our return to the United States, where an entirely now-become-foreign understanding of social structure and social system was in place. Because I had been employed in Germany when and where the accident took place (we had lived there for five years while I worked on my PhD), we paid into the German tax system and therefore were covered under the German social system.

It's nigh impossible for us here in the United States to imagine the different ways in which Germans understand their collective social responsibility. For example, when we lived there everyone had six weeks of vacation. There was an income-adjusted stipend per child to offset the costs associated with children until the age of eighteen. Pregnant women left their work six weeks before the due date and came back eight weeks later—while being paid a substantial portion of their salary. If a woman chose to take a leave of absence after the birth of her child, she was assured that her position, or a position similar to it, would be waiting for her for three years after the birth of that child. Pediatric pharmaceuticals were free until the age of eighteen. Everyone had the option of being covered under a national health insurance plan.

So for all the care that my husband received before he died five hours after the accident, and for all the care my son received until we left to return to the States—the ambulance ride, countless surgeries (including the removal of Karl's skull, the freezing of his skull, the reinsertion of his skull, feeding tubes, and multiple brain shunts), six weeks in ICU, routine MRIs and CT scans, treatment for MRSA, physical and occupational and speech and music therapies, another ambulance ride to a rehabilitation center in the Alps, six weeks of treatment there, more scans, more therapies, not to mention food and housing for even my parents, my daughter, and me—we paid maybe a hundred dollars out of pocket.

A hundred bucks.

When I returned to the States, devastated and exhausted and tired, I couldn't get—or afford—health insurance unless I worked. Never mind that I needed to be working at nothing more than keeping my little boy in the land of the living, keeping my little girl buffered from the angst swirling around her, and keeping my own despair at bay.

Nope.

In Germany—notably with a heritage shaped by Luther's emphasis on grace—you get health care because you are human. Here in the States, you get health care because you have money or a job (though Obamacare helped abate that toxic state of affairs—a policy that, of course, continues to be threatened to varying degrees in multiple places and ways). Even with Obamacare, and certainly without it, access to good insurance can be dependent on what sort of job one holds.

Fortunately, I had been extended a call to teach in a college, so I did have immediate health insurance—in fact, the school generously began that coverage before we even landed, and months before I could work, so that there would be no break in care. That was a powerful gesture of kindness—and yet also a privilege that not many can receive.

Still, due to the intervening accident, the woman the college called to teach was not the woman who arrived on campus. I was beyond depleted and should not have begun to teach as soon as I did. But I did begin teaching, because I so desperately needed health insurance. Yet because I had to work to get health insurance, I couldn't be with my babies during those desperate days. Instead, I had to pay someone else to bring my son to and from his therapies and pay a daycare to care for my girl. Ironically, the cost of health care (even with insurance) and child care, tacked on to the cost of housing and food, were so great that as a single parent I could barely afford to work.

I was positively overwhelmed by the stress of working and single-parenting, of making tough choices about whether I played with my children or cleaned up the dishes or paid the bills or prepped for class or just collapsed to sleep. The simple experience of going grocery shopping while pushing both a cart and a wheelchair while balancing a baby made me weep. I finally settled, during the warmer months anyway, on putting both kids in our Harley Davidson pull-wagon, propping Karl up with shopping bags on the way there and with groceries on the way home, with Else either rolling along on top of or underneath the pile of food and toilet paper.

I will never forget the day that I sat in front of my computer, only two years after getting my PhD, with a tenure-track position at a college in hand, to begin the process of applying for welfare. It had become clear that I could not do it all, and in the process of trying to deny that truth, I was dying another death, this time not from grief but from the pressing weight of finitude.

This wrenching situation, however, began to reveal all sorts of truths from which I had been protected by virtue of birth and fluke. I had benefited from a middle-class educated background, but that did nothing to insulate me from the unwelcome, unbearable onslaught of pain. As a congregational pastor, pre-accident, I had preached Easter with conviction at the bedsides and in the pulpit to those yet in Good Friday, but after the hospital visit or the funeral, I could return to my lifelong experience of Easter, whereas they could not. I had received the call to teach when my family and my spirits were intact—and couldn't maintain the call when, suddenly and randomly, neither were in place. I lived in South Dakota where support for families was (and still is) profoundly lacking. But if I picked up and moved just twenty miles to the east, Minnesota's distinctly different social-systems ethic would provide remarkable respite and relief (which, just over a decade later, proved to be astonishingly true).

Moreover, though, I learned that while privilege couldn't protect me from tragedy, it could buffer me from collateral trauma. For instance, my brother-in-law, for whom I will be forever grateful, is an attorney; he began to wonder whether there were some form of non-retributive financial reparation, perhaps by way of an insurance policy. From his efforts, which I had neither the expertise nor energy nor wherewithal to consider myself, I staved off welfare. I had a system of familial support in place, which provided emotional, logistical, and some measure of financial support if and when needed. I had the education, language, and curated chutzpah to advocate for my family and myself. I had the networked encouragement and, thanks to my brother-in-law's efforts, the resources to identify the possibility of starting first one and then another business as a freelance theologian. And because of all of these pieces converging, just over a decade later I had the strength and the resources—financial, emotional, experiential, relational—to move to Minnesota, where I could find a better place for my children—one with special needs, one gifted—to be raised and for me to be.

It is impossible for me to shake the randomness of both the tragedy and the resources I had available that allowed me to begin to recover—and that others in similar situations do not. It became clear that what happened to us could happen to anyone: as I have often said, the accident—and it was just that, for no one was to blame—happened on a corner we had crossed countless times before.

And while we cannot protect ourselves from the familiar corners in life, metaphorical or real, where random tragedy occurs, we can strive protect ourselves from other forms of pain, the likes of which injustice serves up, often not randomly but systematically.

The accident changed everything.

Not least of all, though, it changed my (lack of) awareness of the Christian call to social justice, to advocacy, to political engagement. There wasn't any forgiveness, per se, that needed to be offered in the traumatic post-accident mix—it really was an accident. But there was ample grief, ample desperation, ample inequities of which I had been blissfully oblivious before they came for me and mine.

And I needed relief immediately—not later, but immediately.

I needed not promises, platitudes, or pep talks, but present help and hope.

And I didn't need to hear about justification, in the moments and months post-accident,

I needed to hear about comfort, relief, and justice.

Thanks to the wrenching experience of the accident, it began to dawn on me that perhaps much of Western theology had not so much missed the boat about the implications of the gospel but had missed that there were bigger boats to have been boarded. The gospel includes the good news that we are justified, of course (for countless reasons and on countless occasions, I have depended on that news both before and after the accident!), but the gospel is so much more than that. The gospel, the news that death does not have the last word, announces that death in all of its forms—personal grief, isolation, despair, sin, as well as systemic inequity, injustice, and apathy—are simply not the agenda of God.

If we are audacious enough to identify ourselves with Jesus's resurrection by claiming the label "Christian," then surely we can't help but be audacious enough to identify ourselves with Jesus's resurrection by rejecting death's power wherever and however it makes itself known.

The accident, then, changed everything for me, and it also, then, led to a realization that something needs to be changed in the church. A reformation is needed and, in fact, is in the offing. We are in a moment when we are being collectively called to realize that the gospel is about more than personal forgiveness, more than going to church, more than believing that Jesus will meet us in heaven. Rather, it is about actively participating in personal and communal repentance, rejecting ways and systems that cause or foster inequity or oppression. In short, it is about believing in and participating in the agenda revealed in the life, death, and resurrection of Jesus.

It took a personal tragedy for me to see it. Trouble is, there are ample tragedies to see, for those who have eyes to notice and a faith to move us to care.

I finish this preface on Good Friday 2019. Today, I have in my mind the image of Peter denying Jesus not once, not twice, but three times, and I have the sound of Peter's weeping in my spirit. It seems that today, then, is a fitting day to mull the truth that when we "other" others, we deny not only their humanity but our very own. Perhaps that is the most important reformation at hand; we are being called to reform our illusion that we are not all made in the image of God.

If that is true, when we deny another's humanity, we deny God.

And we must do other than that.

We are called to do other than that.

We are freed to do other than that.

We can do no other.

Now, on to abundant thanks, for I can do no other than to extend many. First, my editor Scott Tunseth suffered during this book process, I will tell you what, and offered me not so much justice as mercy! Most every form of life's interventions occurred during the creation of this book: my son's beloved Personal Care Assistant moved away, Karl developed a new medical condition related to his TBI, the Spent Dandelion Theological Retreat Center was created, I presented at several synod assemblies and theological convocations in the States and Canada, blizzards caused snow days at home, our dear Danish foreign exchange student Maja arrived, Karl's bus slid precipitously toward our small ravine and got stuck (not his beloved bus driver's fault), daughter Else excelled in speech and debate tournaments both here and away, my family ratcheted up our we-can-do-no-other political engagement in the 2016 and 2018 elections, and I juggled the daily colorful realities of being a single-parent freelance theologian!

Much of this book, then, was written while holding my son's hand in bed when he was sick, and while at the table where I researched and wrote as I played Angry Birds with him (he and I make quite the team), and while driving girls between home and school in Duluth, and while one eye was trained on the television and one ear on NPR for breaking news, and with books and two huge dogs splayed out on the bed in the dark next to my son in the wee, wee hours of the morning when I had the most hope to work with the fewest disruptions!

In other words, this book was not written as timely as was planned and as I had fully intended, nor in the most . . . optimal of scholarly circumstances. All mistakes are mine, and given the above, I have no doubt that there are several! Scott's patience and perseverance were assuredly above the call of duty and his pay grade. If we Lutherans are wrong about grace (and I sincerely hope we are not), and works really do matter, Scott is so in. Heaps of gratitude also to Fortress Press for having the vision for this series, and to Allyce Amidon for her production expertise!

Given the myriad of competing claims in my world, so many people stepped in to help and support during these days: my dear friend Sara, conveniently also my son's school nurse, who comes for weekly wine and processing of the details of our days; Ash, who stepped up to the PCA plate, valiantly and brilliantly taking over the Angry Birds reins (and Wii and Yoda Bad-Lip-Reading videos and T-ball) so I could write; Dode, who is like my own personal fairy godmother, helping me around the house and the property by seeing and doing things that need to be done and yet which constitutionally I can't see or do; and my havens away from beloved hounds and unloved loads of laundry, the Cedar Coffee Company and At Sara's Table, two local haunts with fine food, fine coffee, and fine hospitality regularly extended to a writer who desperately needs a table, coffee, and carbs!

My family, however—my family is the gift beyond measure. My father, George, retired pastor and theologian, has saved my theological and maternal keister on more than one day, and not just when I've been writing this book! His steadfast support and love for my two kids and me manifests itself in a myriad of ways: searching out missing quote references, driving my daughter to early morning speech team buses, taking over Angry Birds for a spell, and reminding me that every day is a day to raise an Akvavit. I am so grateful for him now, and for his witness extended to me at an early age: preaching against an ICBM named "Corpus Christi," marching with clerical collar on in the streets for a nuclear freeze, initiating conversations about whether our congregation was being called to declare itself a sanctuary, and saying, "Sure," when my sister and I asked if we could slap "ERA YES" stickers on our bedroom doors.

Karl wasn't able to smile for the first eight to ten weeks after the accident. It was devastating, for Karl was more or less born beaming. Over the years, he has made up for lost time; now, his regular and quite famous smile could save the world, I am convinced. It has certainly saved mine. His goofy grin shines manifest gladness, manifest grounding, and manifest grace my way.

Else, though—Else was more or less born on fire with righteous indignation, her infant wails screaming out, "This system of birth is outrageous! There must be a better way to make this happen!" She is so bright, winsome, witty, kind, compassionate, convicted, solid, and filled with integrity and hard-won wisdom. As pastoral colleague and friend Brendan said once, "In the name of sweet Jesus, Anna, please tell me you are harnessing her power for good, because if you aren't, we are all doomed."

Every day I tell my children that I am the luckiest mama in the universe, and I mean it.

They define joy for me, joy that is so much different than happiness, or even gladness; it is a way of being, joy is. Karl and Else have had so much of their be-ing threatened with so much in their young lives, and yet they have met each onslaught ultimately with joy. Naturally, they—we—know sadness and anger and loss, but collectively we have come to decide that we refuse to cede death another win by ourselves becoming, in our fundamental essence, sad or angry or lost. And so Karl and Else have defied death with joy, and they have taught me the art of joyful defiance when death taunts. And even when it doesn't.

"Why do you look for the living among the dead? He is not here. He is risen."

Alleluia.

1

I Can Do No Other

I don't believe that there is such a thing as an atheist. That isn't
to say I don't understand what people mean by the term—
namely, someone who believes that there is no God or, to say it
differently, someone who doesn't believe in God. But at the end
of the day, it is not at all clear what, exactly, is being denied. In
what, or in whom, is one not believing? In his *Large Catechism*,
Brother Martin Luther (1483–1546) offers an assist in this explanation to the first commandment, "You shall have no other gods
before me":

> A "god" is the term for that to which we are to look for
> all good and in which we are to find refuge in all need.
> Therefore, to have a God is nothing else than to trust
> and believe in that one with your whole heart. As I have
> often said, it is the trust and faith of the heart alone that
> make both God and an idol. If your faith and trust are
> right, then your God is the true one. Conversely, where

your trust is false and wrong, there you do not have the true God. For these two belong together, faith and God. Anything on which your heart relies and depends, I say, that is really your God.[1]

Now, there's a lot going on here, a lot that we can see all the more clearly if we pay attention to just one word in that text, contextualized by two others that are not in the text and not even in common parlance.

First, the word *trust*. If we trust in something or someone, we believe that the object of our trust deserves our commitment and will not let us down, lead us astray, or abandon us. The word is not to be used lightly, that is. We trust only that which we believe is worthy of our trust. We mistrust that which isn't worthy of our trust.

It seems simple: we sit on (trust) the sturdy chair and avoid (mistrust) the rickety one. But the worthiness of something or someone isn't always so clear. In fact, it is more than just unclear; sometimes discernment of what or who is the trustworthy one can be powerfully difficult. To the rescue come two quite uncommon words, the relevant ones not in Luther's text: *penultimate* and *ultimate*. Although these are not garden-variety, everyday terms, they are positively indispensable for figuring out our trust issues (so to speak) and even for helping us identify God.

In Greek, words have accent marks on certain syllables. It's a grammatical technique that helps determine the meaning, declension, or conjugation of a word. Because English doesn't tend to use accent marks in the same way as Greek does, grasping the importance of a tiny slash is a bit of a stretch. A funny story from my days of teaching religion might help. The class had been studying the apostle Paul and his references to different forms of love in Greek thought. In the text were the Greek words *agape*, as in "generous Christian love," along with *philia* and *eros*, referring to "brotherly love" and "erotic love." Later, in the vocabulary section of the unit's exam, two different students (two!) wrote the definition of *agape* as "mouth wide open." Right. So it's the phonetic difference between the Greek *agape* [agápē] and the English *agape* [ə'gāp]. The words are spelled the same but pronounced differently.

Clearly, accents matter! But who knows where to put them? In Greek, it's by counting your syllables. In Greek grammar, the last syllable of a word is called the *ultimate* syllable: using the word *syl-la-ble* as our working example, *-ble* is the ultimate syllable. The second-to-last syllable of a word is the *penultimate* syllable; in *syllable*, that would be *-la*.

Returning then to Luther's definition of "god," Luther didn't use the words *penultimate* and *ultimate*, but they rest behind his understanding of trust. Luther understood that every single moment, we are trusting in something. As I write, I trust that the chair on which I am sitting will not break; I trust that my two hounds will not escape from their dog run; I trust that I will see my children again after their school; I trust that tomorrow will come. However, the truth is, if I trust my entire life to any of these, I might discover myself being hurt if the chair's legs break, fearful if my dogs go missing, wrenched with grief if something unspeakable happens to my son or daughter, and even perhaps surprised right before existence stops.

You see, it is terrifically easy to trust in something that is penultimate instead of something that is ultimate. There is nothing wrong, of course, with trusting one's chair, one's dog fence, one's children's well-being, and even tomorrow's arrival. But if our entire essence were dependent on these realities being always true, and if for any reason they became *not* true, then we would learn that we had placed our trust in the *pen*ultimate rather than the *ul*timate—namely, in the thing right before the last thing, rather than the last thing.

We can see trust play out in any number of ways: benign, blessed, and nefarious. On the one hand, we trust in love, we trust that we have a job, we trust in democracy; on the other, perhaps we trust in alcohol to numb us, in lying to protect ourselves, in gossip to entertain us, or in beauty to keep us ageless. Any objects of our trust, even the ones that seem to be good, could—and often do—let us down. Loves die, employers downsize, and governments are overthrown.

> It is terrifically easy to trust in something that is penultimate instead of something that is ultimate.

Regardless, the point is this: at any given time, we are trusting in *something*. We all have a god. Something receives our momentary commitment; whatever that is becomes our god. It is the thing to which we say yes, because we believe that it says yes to us. The question, then, isn't whether we have a god. The questions are which god we have and whether our god is ultimate or penultimate. It matters, because whatever we trust determines how we live.

To circle back to Luther, then, we see that Luther did not define God as "Father, Son, Holy Spirit." No, instead God is "that to which we are to look for all good and in which we are to find refuge in all need." In other words, our God is that one above and beyond all others, in which we place our ultimate trust. The first commandment makes it clear that even God knew there are options. The commandment is "You shall have no other gods but me," not "There are no other gods but me."

Any number of ideas, material goods, or people can claim our allegiance and thereby become our god. For that reason, there isn't such a thing as an atheist: everybody trusts in something every moment. Again, the question isn't whether you believe in god. The question is rather in *which* god, or gods, or God you believe.

This book is born out of the conviction that currently, at least two gods are competing for our collective trust: nationalism (and its many sub-manifestations) and quietism. Both make a case for and a claim on our allegiance; each draws on different motivations of institutional protectionism and self-protection. I am convinced that the primary issue facing the church these days is born out of a first-commandment question: Who, or what, is our God, and—to complete this question in a way that can't really be more Lutheran—what does that mean?

If we say we trust in something, we act accordingly. If I didn't trust my chair, say, I wouldn't sit in it. Because I do trust it,

I'm happily—and presumably safely—perched while I type out these thoughts. I let my children go to school because it is as safe a place as it can be, and they love to learn. I have walked along our dog run and know that although, on occasion, the hounds might get stuck *in* the fence, they can't get *out* of it. And I have decided to err on the side of Luther and plant an apple tree (or, in my case, order seeds just today for our spring garden) even though the world might end tomorrow. Likewise, if we say we trust in God, then we act accordingly.

The radical question being asked today of those who descend from Luther's Reformation is this: What are the implications of trusting in God today, in our context?

In many ways, it's the same question Luther asked in his day. But I'm of the mind that the crucial and most pressing answer to that question is markedly different than what it was when Martin Luther started wondering about faith, theology, and life in and outside of the church, because the context of five hundred years ago is vastly different from ours. Then, Luther pointed at indulgences as a primary offense against the gospel. Indulgences were sold by the church in exchange for eternal forgiveness. But the notion that one could buy one's way out of sins was, indeed, nothing less than extortion, and worse, it taught that our standing before God depends on whether we are spiritually or financially worthy.

Now, however, the context has changed. While many believers do still fear that their unrighteousness is more powerful than God's righteousness, new existential anxieties have arisen. In a day and age when globalization, polarization, racism, bigotry, sexism, gender discrimination, economic disparity, and environmental collapse frame not just our news but our very lives, people are yearning to know something else: Does God, and does the church, care? Will the church built on the foundation of justification by grace stand for justice in the world?

> Will the church built on the foundation of justification by grace stand for justice in the world?

This book addresses these contemporaneous theological, spiritual, ecclesial, cultural, and political questions and does so by way of theology and history:

- First, to lay the framework of thought, we will delve into who Jesus was and how our claim that he died and was raised establishes our faith and affects the way we live it out.
- Second, we will pay attention to Luther's context and his theology, juxtaposing it with our present context, five hundred years hence.
- Third, we will venture into a review of expressions of courage and action born precisely out of faith, lingering especially on recent examples of Nazi resistance, liberation theology, black and womanist theology, and feminist theology, each of which comes at social justice in its unique ways and yet shares a common conviction that justice work is central to the Christian life.
- Fourth, we will observe how our faith grounding and our faith history weave together and entwine themselves

into our present moment, offering both warnings and encouragement in these new days.

■ Last, based on these explorations, we make a case that justice, anchored in justification, is our new Reformation moment—one not inconsistent with Luther's theology but weighted differently and segmented broadly to address the different concerns that claim our day.

Discussion Questions

1. What do you think the author is saying about "ultimate trust"? How do we sometimes place our trust in penultimate things?

2. The author states on page 6, "The radical question being asked today of those who descend from Luther's Reformation is this: What are the implications of trusting in God today, in our context?" What are your initial thoughts in response to her question?

3. What other key questions does the author raise in this introduction? What are your intial reactions to these questions?

4. The author hints at the need for a new Reformation moment in the church. Before you read further, how might you describe what such a moment looks like?

2

Here I Stand

In the summer of 2016, my two children and I moved to Two Harbors, Minnesota, just about twenty-five miles north of Duluth. My vocation as a freelance theologian allows us to plant our stakes most anywhere. One day, in early 2016, I asked my daughter (then thirteen) where, if she could choose, our next home should be. She first suggested that she could happily pitch darts at a map and decide that way, and I replied yes, that would be adventuresome, but perhaps we could come up with a more methodical approach. Else thought for a moment and said it would be quite fine to live in a place with woods, hills, and lots and lots of water. Without knowing it, she described Minnesota's North Shore, so now here we are, as happy as can be.

Though we've been here for close to three years now, I still can't believe I get to hear the foghorns of the freighters, watch them at the Two Harbors docks gracefully navigate between breakwall and shore, and see the enormous ships just off the bay when I pull out of my driveway and hang a right. (Else doesn't roll her eyes at me very often at all, but she is now fairly over my "Hello, ore boat!" greeting to these magnificent ships in the early mornings when we leave for school.)

In late 2016, I posted on my Facebook page two or three pictures of some of these tankers anchored just off of the Two Harbors docks. Enormous though they were, one could barely see them through the low, dense fog. I wrote (and, granted, it was a bit over the top):

> My Danish grandma called similar mists over the North Sea *hekse brygge*, namely "witches' brew." Yesterday, Dad and I were indeed bewitched . . . and really glad that instead of being on the deck of one of these frozen phantom-like tankers at the Two Harbors docks, we could hop right back into the heated seats of my Subaru and speed right on home to our stove.

Not long after that, but long enough so that I didn't make the connection, a very odd message request showed up in my Facebook inbox. It was from a man I did not know, who asked, simply, "So. Have you ever been on an ore boat?"

Needless to say, I found that not a little creepy. Wanting to be charitable but also not a sheer idiot, I googled his name before I replied to him. I discovered that my now-friend James was, of all things, once a Lutheran (ELCA) pastor, but he had quit professional ministry to become instead a first mate on an ore boat. As luck and coincidence would have it, he and his wife are based in Duluth. Somehow, my post had been marked as public, so he had seen it, and it took him only a few nanoseconds after our meeting to suggest that perhaps my view of life on an ore boat was a bit romanticized.

After a couple of messages back and forth, James invited my daughter and me to tour his ore boat, the *Roger Blough*. It was thrilling: these freighters are all the more impressive up close. One of the highlights of our tour was seeing the taconite pellets tumble out of the dock chutes and into the boat. First the ore is loaded on one side, and then the tanker backs up and sails around to the other side of the dock. Then it's filled up with the ore on the opposite side.

While the pellets spilled into the ship, James told Else and me to keep an eye on five lights at the bow and the stern of the ship. The outer four are red, and the middle one is white. If one or two of the red lights are lit on either side, it's an alert that the ship is listing; that is, it isn't evenly balanced. But when both white lights, bow and stern, are illuminated, the crew is assured that the cargo is equally distributed in all the bays. Until that happens, the mates holler out, "She's not trimmed to the white light!"

As soon as James told us that phrase, I burst out laughing. "That," I gasped, "would be a great insult directed at me on most days!—'Folks, she's not trimmed to the white light!'"

I am many things. Balanced is not one of them.

It is a small but real comfort to know I'm not alone! Fact is, I don't know many people who are perfectly balanced and don't have a metaphorical red light (or two) beaming out an alert on their bow, their stern, or both ends! Yet a myth we hear all the time is that we are to live a balanced life. It is actually possible, says the nasty rumor, to be balanced. But the pursuit of "living a balanced life" is impossible because we are finite. We simply cannot attend to all of the necessary claims life makes upon us. And sometimes, the claims upon us—even right and noble ones—compete or cause friction.

For example, so that I could meet the very appropriate deadline for this book, my son, to whom I am committed above all as a mother and who suffered a traumatic brain injury at a very young age, had to sit beside me and play by himself, not just for a day or two, but for many days on end, while I furiously pursued my research and writing. My son deserved to have his mama play Angry Birds with him, and my editor deserved to have this manuscript. Both were true, but fulfilling both obligations couldn't happen at the same time. From another angle, our faith calls us to certain ways of being in the world—ways that run contrary to notions of patriotism or understandings of national loyalty that also may call to us.

> We simply cannot attend to all of the necessary claims life makes upon us.

In either case, we have every reason to feel imbalanced. The simultaneous call to vocation and to family responsibilities tugged at me from opposite directions, and I was listing. Likewise, we declare our allegiance to God yet feel some commitment, even pressure to pledge our commitment, also to the flag, a symbol that might represent values that are inconsistent with God, and we list. Under those circumstances, to use "balance" as a gauge might leave us feeling all the more *im*balanced.

I have come, instead, to appreciate the call to live an *integrated* life. I like the word *integrated* very much. It suggests that if you are integrated, you are aware of, make use of, and respect all of the *integers* of your life, and you live with *integrity* in the sense of being complete and sound. When we live a well-integrated life, then, we acknowledge that what we are doing might *look* like we are not balanced and might indicate that we are not balanced, but we are, in fact and at least, living with *integrity*.

Interestingly, the Judeo-Christian tradition offers a faith word that corresponds quite nicely to the metaphor of being "trimmed to the white light" while also helping us think about living with integrity. That word is *righteousness*. The Hebrew word for righteous is *tzadek*. If we are *tzadek*, we act in keeping with God's ways and laws. But *tzadek* has another meaning, too. The beloved late Lutheran theologian Joseph Sittler (1904–1987) tells of his car breaking down in Israel. When he went to pick it up from the repair shop, the mechanic declared that his vehicle was, of all things, *tzadek*! In this case, *tzadek* meant properly aligned. The car's integrity had been compromised by some bumpy roads in Jerusalem, but once it had been realigned, it was again righteous.[1]

Every day, Christians are implicitly and explicitly asked these questions: To what should we be properly aligned? By what is our integrity threatened? How can we (again and again) be trimmed to the white light? In short, what is our God, and what does it mean to claim that one as our God?

Christians claim that we understand God revealed through the gospel of Jesus. This is an answer to the question, to be sure.

Despite our ready use of the word *gospel*, however, there isn't actually a consensus about what the gospel is, means, or implies. It is often said that the gospel is that God loves us or that the gospel is the forgiveness of sins. I think both of these are true; that is, I do believe that God is love, and I do believe that our sins are forgiven. However, thanks to my late mentor Lutheran theologian Walter Bouman (1927–2005), I do not believe that either of these sayings really defines the gospel. Both are assertions. They are opinions. They are ideas. But in order to be believed, they require some historical grounding, some reason that one should commit to these notions as truth. (To illustrate, we could say that God is, perhaps, a banana, but such a statement clamors for some substantial reason why we should throw our lives to a God in the form of a long, yellow, smushy fruit.)

The notion of gospel has to be anchored in an event; even the Greek word for gospel—namely, *euangellion*—makes that very case. The prefix *eu-* means good; think, for example of *euthanasia*, which means good death, or *euphemism*, which means good speech, or *eulogy*, a good word (and sometimes euphemisms are employed during eulogies!). The second part of the word, *-angellion*, might be easier for us to see straight away; it serves also as the root word for *angel*, which means messenger. So, quite literally, the word *euangellion* means good message or, as we might be more accustomed to hearing it, good news. Sometimes we hear a term so often that it's easy to forget its import. That could well be the case of the "good news," the English translation of the Greek word for gospel. The gospel is news, and it is good news.

But "news" is something that happened. Furthermore, news is something that affects you. For you, as a reader of this book, it is not news that, as I write, the snow on my metal roof is melting at an alarmingly fast rate. To anyone standing under the eaves, though, it could well be news—really cold, wet, heavy news! Yet, as newsy as it is to a person visiting my home as I write, it will not be news to anyone by the time this book is published. Either the snow will be melted, and thoughts will have turned to snow cones instead of snow shoveling, or else we will have new snows drifting along our drive. That is, while the snow slabs racing down onto the sidewalks is newsy to those of us at 808 Stanley in the *moment*, it isn't going to be news for much longer than today, given the warm temperatures that will melt away the white stuff by midafternoon.

However, Christians say the gospel is news that wasn't just news back in the days of Jesus and his first followers. No, we audaciously say the gospel is still news—and *good* news at that. So, what then is this news, this *good* news? What is the gospel?

The good news, the *euangelion*, the gospel, is that Jesus is risen. The dead guy didn't stay dead, as dead people are typically wont to do.

> We audaciously say the gospel is still news—and *good* news at that.

That's it. That's the crux, so to speak, of the gospel: resurrection, life out of death.

Furthermore, Christians assert that the gospel, the good news, is not life just for Jesus. This resurrection event wasn't just a personal triumph for him. No, resurrection means life out of death is offered to *all* people. The Christian gospel is news for all people, still, even more than two thousand years later.

Besides *righteousness* and *gospel*, another faith vocabulary word needs reflection, and it's a common one used so freely that we might not notice its internal power and significance: *Christian*. Isn't it interesting that, although we speak of Jesus on a regular basis, although we say we believe in Jesus, although we say that Jesus died for our sins, we do not call ourselves "Jesus-ians"? Instead, we refer to our religious faith and tradition as *Christ*ian. That's worth a linger. We are Christians, and not Jesusians, because we believe that Jesus is the *Christ*.

That word matters. It flows off of our tongues so readily right after "Jesus" that we might even halfway think that Christ is Jesus's last name, as if Mary Christ and Joseph Christ had a sweet little swaddled baby named Jesus Christ. Of course, that is not at all the case. Instead, the word *Christ* is a title. A title isn't something one claims but is rather something bestowed, as in the case of such titles as hero, doctor, mother, plumber, and congresswoman. Christ is a title that informs the hearer that something is unique about this man named Jesus. He is a specific man named Jesus, but the term *Christ* refers to something beyond that man Jesus.

Jesus is the Christ because we believe that he is the Messiah. The word *Christ* comes from the Greek word *Christos*. That word means anointed and is itself a translation of the Hebrew word *mashiach*, or in its English form, messiah. Notice, for example, that embedded in the terms we customarily use to designate eras, you find somewhat hidden attestations that Jesus is Lord. BC abbreviates "Before Christ," and AD shortens "Anno Domini," namely "Year of Our Lord" in Latin. When, say, journalists reference something occurring in 150 BC, they are making an implicit, and possibly inadvertent, faith claim, for BC marks not Jesus's life as a man but Jesus's role as Messiah. For this reason, out of respect for people who are not Christian, many historians and theologians change BC to BCE (Before the Common Era) and AD to CE (Common Era).

It is a clue to the early Christian understanding of the significance of Jesus and no coincidence that all evidence suggests Jesus was called the Christ primarily after he was risen. That's a crucial piece, because it indicates that his resurrection confirmed belief among the early believers that Jesus was, in fact, the Messiah, the Christ. Note that after his disciples came to believe that Jesus was no longer dead, they identified him with Yahweh by worshipping him (Matt 28:17), praying to him (1 Cor 1:2; Acts 7:59), proclaiming salvation in his name (Acts 4:11–12), addressing hymns about and to him (Phil 2:6–11; Rev 5:9–10), offering that signs are done in his name (Acts 3:6), baptizing in his name (Acts 8:16), and not least of all, addressing him as God (Rom 9:5; Col 1:15; 2:2, 9).

All of these texts point to the early conviction that Jesus is God, that Jesus is the Messiah. And again, why? Because, despite the general tendency for dead people to stay dead, Jesus didn't. The early believers determined that this resurrection was *euangellion*, was good news, was the gospel. Moreover, they believed that the resurrection confirmed that what Jesus was up to is what

God is up to. That is, they were convinced that Jesus's agenda reflects God's agenda.

What if the one who was raised had mocked and belittled, excluded and assaulted, created barriers between people, and dealt in the ways of hate, bullying, and death? If that sort of leader had been raised, our understanding of the term *Christ* would compel us to very different conclusions about God's notion of *messiah*, the nature of God's agenda, and God's expectations of faithfulness according to this kind of agenda. However, Jesus's life and death reveal quite a specific impression of God's intention for this world and for those who identify themselves as followers of God, one which contrasts not only with the alter-ego messiah just described but with the ways of the world. Jesus engaged in activities like healing and feeding, welcoming and teaching, and extending—even breaking—boundaries, drinking good wine and eating good food, and of course, forgiving. It's a critical, if obvious, detail to note: the resurrection confirms that Jesus's agenda was God's agenda, so it simultaneously reveals who God is and reminds us of who we are to be.

> **Jesus's agenda reflects God's agenda.**

My opening tale of the ore boat's first mate intent on keeping the boat trimmed to the white light in order to sail true serves up a fine metaphor for people of faith. The light to which we are to be trimmed shines from the empty tomb, shedding light onto Jesus's life and ministry, not just as example, but as the very expression of God's will for our world. That light illuminates the way of those who identify as followers of God and as Christians.

Here, then, is an opportunity to ask a very Lutheran sort of question: What does this *euangellion*, this good news, this resurrection event mean to us as individuals, as members of the church, and as those who are called to let the light shine into the world? Perhaps the best response to this question comes from Bouman, who frequently said, "Now that you know that death doesn't win, there is more to do with your lives than preserve them." Now that you know that death doesn't win, there is more to do with your lives than preserve them. Bouman is referring to a ridiculously radical freedom that this *euangellion*, this good news, this resurrection offers us. The truth is, we can readily imagine any number of motivations to preserve our lives, for any number of reasons could explain why we are afraid we might *need* to preserve our lives: the possibility of being attacked in body or spirit, being alone, being exposed, being ill, being mortal, being vulnerable, being in love, not being in love, being a single parent, losing our reputation, our families, and our privilege. Were any of these things come to pass, it would be a death of some sort. Implicitly, I believe that even the New Testament writers understood the truth that we see reasons to fear. Particularly in the Gospel of Luke, we hear prophets, angels, and Jesus himself announcing that we do not need to be afraid. Such a reassurance wouldn't need to be offered if people weren't afraid in the first place! But Jesus's resurrection reminds us that death does not have the last word. As I have come to say, the gospel promises us that death is real but life is realer. It is into this sort of promise that we are baptized.

Baptizo means, in Greek, to immerse. When I moved to Sioux Falls, I observed a plant in our yard that was beautiful for about a week and then became all sprawly and awkward, like an adolescent. During that week of beauty, gorgeous shoots of purple flowers burst forth from the stems extending from the center. I called it, not particularly originally, That Purple Plant. A friend and his wife came over when That Purple Plant was really showing its stuff. It was very purple, and it was very proud of being purple. It defined purpletude. And my friend said, as naturally as could be, "Baptisia! Huh. I didn't know it grew here in South Dakota."

It turns out that That Purple Plant had a real name, which of course he knew (he taught Greek). It's related to the Greek word from which we get *baptism*, because those gorgeous purple leaves make a powerful dye. The leaves dye the heck out of things—fabric, skin, paper. The dyed items become purple *forever*. Likewise, when we are baptized, we are also dyed in a sense. We are marked by the cross of Christ—*forever*.

We are immersed into the promise that nothing, not even fear, and not even death, is more powerful than God's love for us. Interestingly, while the primary theological motivation for baptizing babies is an assertion of grace (God's love is pure gift; simply by being alive, we are worthy of receiving grace), sometimes people baptize out of fear of death. Emergency baptisms, for example, take place to stave off damnation in case of the baby's death before the child is baptized. Even the sacrament of baptism, you see, can represent our fear, not least of all fear of judgment and death, rather than our trust in a living grace-filled God.

However, left only with the *act* of baptism, without knowledge either of the event or of a community that nurtures a life lived out of it or action born out of it, we have, essentially, only a lovely piece of paper taped to our back—one that we can't see, but God can, that says, "Baptized!" But if we belong to a community, or if we are in a family that knows and embraces our baptism, then that piece of paper is brought from behind our back and is taped to our fronts, smack dab on our foreheads.

In our family, Else, Karl, and I have morning blessings and evening blessings. Our nightly blessings begin just before the children fall asleep. The first goes something like this: "Sweet one, are you comfy? Are you cozy? Are you content? Do you know that you are loved?" And they answer yes (or Karl will often say, with a grin, "Nope"). When we finally get through the questions and answers, we will say together, after they let me know they are loved, "That is the *most important thing.*" Then I move into the second and final ritual with both K and E. It's especially important to me, because I began it while little Karl was struggling in the intensive care unit after his traumatic brain injury. I say, "Sweet child, you are beautiful, you are safe, and I love you." And then, as I make the sign of the cross on their foreheads, I say, "And so does God." When she was just a tiny toddler, daughter Else started to make the sign of the cross on my forehead, and to this day, she still does.

It is crucial to me that my children know that they are, no matter what, loved. And I want them to realize that just as their grandfather and father made the sign of the cross on their foreheads when they were baptized (and had it made on *their* foreheads, too, decades and decades before), so it can be made on their foreheads every single day, reminding them that they are *ultimately* claimed by the Father, and the Son, and the Holy Spirit. Everything else is penultimate.

You see, as Bouman taught many of us, baptism only "works" if it is "used," that is, if it is trusted. Our God is that in which or in whom we trust. Baptism initiates us into a life of trust in God, of our participation in the community of God, into the risen Jesus. The word *community* is key here, for baptism is not only an individual matter. It is, of course, a promise to each individual person (we are known by name). But baptism initiates us into the community of the baptized. We are, in a sense, baptized into a community of trusters.

> We are, in a sense, baptized into a community of trusters.

This is good news that radiates out of the good news: We don't go at it alone. We live and worship with people who collectively commit their lives to the notion that life is more powerful than death, who make the conscious decision not to trust fear, and who believe that because Jesus is risen, we will live as people claimed by the resurrection promise. Now that we know that death doesn't win, there is more to do with our lives than preserve them.

It is worth noting that the Old Germanic and Saxon root of the word *believe* means to hold dear, to love, to care, to desire. We are what we trust. Therefore, if we believe in the risen Jesus—the raised one who spent his life healing the sick, serving the poor, teaching the crowds, feeding the hungry, forgiving the sinners, and welcoming the outcasts—we become ambassadors of that Jesus. We become incarnate gospel, we become tangible grace, and we become palpable hope, because we are what we hold dear— namely, we are what we love, care about, desire, and believe.

I have often said that it is deeply unfortunate that in our common creeds (not least of all, the one uttered during baptismal services!), Jesus jumps from Mary's arms into the arms of Pontius Pilate. Why is that? What is missed? Simply, Jesus's life of service—his healing and serving and teaching and feeding and forgiving and welcoming. At one level, it is no wonder we don't emphasize his life. It certainly puts a crimp in one's evangelism campaign: Come! Heal, feed, forgive, welcome, die! Services at nine o'clock.

However, were we to evangelize (the verb related to *euangellion*, or good news) in this way, we would be truthful. That is, to be a Christian disciple means that everything that we do emanates from our core identity, from our core teacher, our core rabbi, our core Christ. Everything.

Episcopalian theologian John Westerhoff (1933–) once said that stewardship is what we do after we say we believe.[2] One could say the same about discipleship: discipleship is what we do after we say we believe. Put another way, our identity as disciples is defined by what or whom we trust, or in what or in whom we place our allegiance.

In a striking way, a conflict about the pledge of allegiance to the flag is a case about discipleship. When my daughter was seven, Else announced that she had decided to refuse to say the pledge in school. "Why, baby girl?" I asked, both struck by the courage of this tiny thing and reaching for my seat belt in anticipation of her teenage years. "Because," she said, "there clearly *isn't* justice and liberty for all, and I don't think it's right to pledge allegiance to anything but God."

> Discipleship is what we do after we say we believe.

Now, if one feels some offense by my daughter's decision, let me be clear: my daughter and I are not anti-American. We are, however, against the myth that the United States should receive our allegiance, because it (like anything less than God) can act against God's will.

That said, some research about the pledge has helped us reframe our objections. It turns out that the pledge was written by a man named Francis Bellamy (1855–1931), who was a Baptist minister and a Christian socialist. In 1891, Bellamy was hired by a man named Daniel Sharp Ford, who owned a small printed magazine called the *Youth's Companion*. The journal's sales were slumping, so Ford and Bellamy came up with an idea to bump up subscriptions by tying them to a donation of a flag to every school. A year later, subscriptions were down again, so a new idea was hatched: yoke the subscriptions with the four hundredth anniversary of Christopher Columbus's arrival. For this ploy, Bellamy crafted not only a flag but also a pledge and a salute. It's worth noting that although we know this salute now as a hand on the heart, originally it was an arm and a hand extended in the air. It is also worth noting that it wasn't until about sixty years later that the phrase "under God" was added as an antidote to a fear—a fear of communism bearing down upon American society.[3]

Bellamy believed heartily that ordinary people were threatened by the wealthy class and by corporations, so he sought to encourage the development of economic justice by large government, and he insisted that Christians are called to live their lives in society as did Jesus. (It's not coincidental that Bellamy began his career as a preacher, but after several years of service, he was ousted by a congregation that disliked his tendency to describe Jesus as a socialist!) Interestingly, then, when one understands the origin of the Pledge of Allegiance, one realizes that the *point* of the pledge was to make our nation emulate Jesus's callings to protect the poor and the weak. It is possible, then, to pledge allegiance to that vision.

To pledge allegiance to the *flag*, however, raises some questions, for Christians are called not to be disciples of the flag, but rather disciples of Jesus, who espoused views that may run quite contrary to national commitments. The church is called to be an ambassador of salvation to all people, not just to those who are citizens of the United States of America.

So here is another word that deserves some reflection: *salvation*. It, too, is best understood if we look at the Greek word from which it is translated, *soteria*, which means health, healing, and wholeness. While the word's origins are about health, healing, and wholeness, the English word *salvation* often finds itself used in this way: "Are you saved?" The implication is anything but health, healing, and wholeness. Rather, in a stunningly efficient way, this three-word question transforms the *euangellion*, the gospel, the good news, into crushingly bad news. It becomes a threat. Salvation has come to mean this: "Have you accepted Jesus Christ as your personal Lord and Savior? Because if you haven't, you will be damned to hell when you die."

That's not what Scripture reveals about how Jesus used or understood the word. "Today," we hear in Luke 19:9, "salvation has come to this house." Jesus did not announce here that the hearers were about to die and discover whether their "acceptance" cut the eternal mustard. Instead, Jesus meant that in him, one finds health, healing, and wholeness. Jesus wanted to convey that in him they would *live*, and live in a new way, in a way defined not by the world, but by the news that Jesus is risen. You see, with this understanding of the Greek word for salvation, when we hear "Are you saved?" instead of hearing a *threat*, we can hear questions of care and concern: "Are you well? Are you healed? Are you whole? For if not, how can I be Jesus to you?" That, you see, is being a baptized disciple: How can I be an ambassador of *soteria*, of salvation, of health, healing, and wholeness, of resurrection to you?

Bouman brought to my attention Tom Stoppard's play *Rosencrantz and Guildenstern Are Dead*. It's the tale of Hamlet told from the perspective of two peripheral characters, Hamlet's friends Rosencrantz and Guildenstern. In it, one discovers a marvelous passage, a heartbreaking passage, of actors whom Rosencrantz and Guildenstern ditched in the woods as the troupe was performing a play. When the actors reconvene with these two young men at Elsinore, the lead actor speaks the following passage:

> You don't understand the humiliation of it—to be tricked out of a single assumption, which makes our existence viable—that somebody is watching. . . . The plot was two corpses gone before we caught sight of ourselves, stripped naked in the middle of nowhere and pouring ourselves down a bottomless well. . . . There we are—demented children mincing about in clothes that no one ever wore, speaking as no man ever spoke, swearing love in wigs and rhymed couplets, killing each other with wooden swords, hollow protestations of faith hurled after empty promises of vengeance—and every gesture, every pose, vanishing into the thin unpopulated air. We ransomed our dignity to the clouds, and the uncomprehending birds listened. Don't you see?! We're actors—we're the opposite of people! . . . We're actors. . . . We pledged our identities, secure in the conventions of our trade; that someone would be watching. And then, gradually, no one was.[4]

Bouman used the text to get at the feelings of abandonment we would feel if we were to learn, or at the very least believe, that there is no God watching. He was speaking as a product of the twentieth century, when the postwar questions of existentialism and nihilism commanded people's attention: Does God exist, and does it matter anyway? Stoppard's passage is a powerful tool in that way. But it can also be used to demonstrate how people feel if the church, the purported incarnate presence of God, looks away, doesn't notice the action in people's lives, the drama within them, the solitude of suffering, the helplessness of powerlessness.

We can't ask, "Are you well?" if we aren't watching people's plays, aren't watching their lives—not watching in the sense of popping corn before tuning in to a voyeuristic episode of *Big Brother*, but watching in the sense of noticing. In John 5:1–10, Jesus noticed the man who had been ill for thirty-eight years, and then he healed him. In Mark 10, Jesus noticed that the disciples were preventing the children from coming to him, and then he welcomed them. In Luke 19:5, Jesus noticed the tax collector Zacchaeus, and then he engaged him. In Luke 14, Jesus noticed that guests were choosing "places of honor," and then he taught them another way. And in Luke 7, he noticed a grieving widow and mother, and then he resuscitated her son. That is, Jesus didn't walk by, Jesus didn't ignore, but rather, Jesus committed himself to the salvation of these people. It is into such a life that Christians are baptized.

All of these people (and so many more in Scripture) were desperate, despairing of their circumstances and any chance of improvement. The root of the word *despair* means to have no hope. They had, that is, no reason to hope. In a book entitled *Eschatology and Hope*, Roman Catholic author Anthony Kelly

(1938–) writes that hope "begins where optimism reaches the end of its tether. Hope stirs when the secure system shows signs of breaking down. Hope is at home in the world of the unpredictable where no human logic or expectation is in control. It rejects any easy assurances of pretending to manage what in fact intrinsically resists management. It relies on something that comes from outside the system."[5] That's a powerful distinction: optimism expresses confidence in something that is entirely possible to come to pass. So, for example, I am optimistic that I will see my son after school today. Hope, however, trusts something that is beyond a realistic expectation. In my case, I am optimistic that I will see my son after school today. I am hopeful that he will walk off the bus to greet me.

> Hope, however, trusts something that is beyond a realistic expectation.

Another way of demonstrating the vast difference between hope and optimism is by way of looking at their opposites. The opposite of optimism is pessimism. The opposite of hope is despair. That's precisely where so many of God's people linger—in despair. They, we, despair that things can't be different, that life is as it will be, that oppression and suffering and poverty and powerlessness win and always will. Worse, sometimes it seems as if this state of matters is condoned by God and even orchestrated by God. Language such as "God's plan" only enables this sort of resignation: "This must be God's plan," or "It's all part of God's plan."

But as has been said after the Holocaust, anything that is said about God has to be said in Auschwitz with the ashes of Jews falling on one's shoulders. And if it cannot be said there, it should not be said anywhere. Can we stand in Auschwitz and say that the assassination of millions of innocent victims was part of God's plan? Can we stand in the streets of Flint, Michigan, and say that the poisoning of their water is God's plan? Can we stand in the schools where mass shootings have taken place and say that the killing of children is part of God's plan? Can we stand in the poverty-ravaged hills of Appalachia and say that their destitution is part of God's plan? Can we stand in the melting snows of the North Pole and say that the disintegration of ancient glaciers due to preventable global warming is part of God's plan? Can we stand in the boardrooms of large corporations and say that the disproportionate wealth given to the privileged elite while the workers in the factories labor at paltry hourly wages with inadequate benefits is part of God's plan? Can we say that the lack of access to affordable health care for all people in the richest nation of the world is part of God's plan?

No. But there is an alternative framework, one that is far more resonant to the will and ways of God, and that is the notion of God's agenda. What is God's agenda? Thankfully, we know it because we have heard the good news: Jesus is risen. The one who fed, healed, welcomed, taught, and forgave—this one did not stay dead. The one who is raised is the Christ and brings salvation into the world—not the sort of salvation that is bad news, that we have to wait to die to receive (only if we have "accepted Jesus Christ as our personal Lord and Savior"). I'm referring to the sort that offers health, healing, and wholeness now—immediate healing and feeding and forgiving and welcoming and hope.

To this point, there is one more key word for us to know as we venture into the notion of a new Reformation moment for the people of God: *prolepsis*. It's not a word that one hears every Sunday, even though I would like to make the case that one should! *Prolepsis* means in Greek a "taking beforehand," an anticipation of that which is yet to come. Christians are called to anticipate the resurrection by representing it by, as has been said, being ambassadors of it.

For example, when a woman discovers that she is pregnant, her life changes. The thing that is promised to come is not yet here but is very much on its way. So although there is no child in her arms, there is a child in her mind and heart. Therefore, eating habits change, furniture arrangements change, and even job commitments change, for the one who is not yet here is coming. Or as I have said to college students, if you are at a party and someone catches your eye, and this someone comes over and asks if you'd be available for a phone call the next day at five o'clock, you will make sure that you are not far removed from your phone beginning as early as 3:32. In either case, one's life is changed by the promise of something greater than the present moment. In the meantime, you prepare the way.

> *Prolepsis* means in Greek a "taking beforehand," an anticipation of that which is yet to come.

Once a Christian begins to grasp the implications of living proleptically, one begins to see one's presence and calling in the world soteriologically—that is, through the lens of *soteria*, of salvation. One cannot simply turn away or be unmoved by injustice, any more than Jesus could be. We, like him and because of him, first notice suffering and then become ambassadors of salvation. As religion professor John Shelley wrote in the preface to Dorothee Sölle's book *Political Theology*, "Thus the question of meaning—"What do we mean when we speak of God?"—must be supplemented by the more practical question: 'What are the social and political consequences of speaking of God, or remaining silent in a particular situation?'"[6]

We notice suffering and we seek to end it, for we are baptized members of the messianic community, of the community of Christ. We are Christians, called therefore to be ambassadors of Christ and of all that his resurrection confirmed: healing, feeding, serving, welcoming, teaching, and forgiving. We are therefore called not to be ambassadors of optimism, but of Easter, of life out of death, of tangible hope.

Discussion Questions

1. The author uses the example of an ore boat being "trimmed to the white light." What does this mean? What might a life "trimmed to the white light" look like?
2. On page 13, the author poses a series of four questions that Christians are explicitly and implicitly asked. How

would you respond at this time to at least one of the questions? Discuss with two others in your group.

3. How does the author define the *euangellion* (the gospel, the good news)? What is its core message? What does this good news mean for those who are called to let the light shine in the world?

4. What meanings can be given to the Greek word *soteria* and the way the English translation, *salvation,* is commonly used in our culture? How does the author compare and contrast these terms? In your opinion, do these terms have more to do with the future or the present? Why?

5. On page 32, John Shelley is quoted as saying, "Thus the question of meaning—'What do we mean when we speak of God?'—must be supplemented by the more practical question: 'What are the social and political consequences of speaking of God, or remaining silent in a particular situation?'" How would you answer these questions?

3

Here He Stood

I was an English major in college, which required a course on poetry. Studying poetry was one thing. I loved the way that these word-artists could communicate the sublime, the noble, the wrenching, the ordinary in ways that made me not just read their poems but feel them. However, the *writing* of poetry was something entirely different. I was positively lousy at it.

One morning, I dragged myself to class, having been up all night trying to write the required assignment: a love poem. Empty-handed and feeling empty-minded, I went up to the professor (the esteemed late Paul Gruchow) to confess that I hadn't been able to come up with a single novel thing to write about love, the assigned topic of the day. Even my analogy of the experience was tired: writing it was like trying to draw blood from a stone. He grinned quietly and said, also quietly, "Yes, Ms. Madsen, love's been done before."

In a very similar way, I realize that Luther has been done before. But a review of Luther, calibrated to the questions of social justice in our immediate context, helps us notice some new moments, new themes, and new cues in Luther's history that invite us to reconsider the theological contribution he could make to this new moment five hundred years down the road.

Just as no one-to-one comparison with Luther's cultural and religious circumstances exists, so is there no one-to-one relationship between his primary theological contributions and those we need today. Put another way, just as we don't wander our streets in fifteenth-century garb (at least not without a couple of sideways glances), we can't simply take Luther's on-the-cusp-of-modern theology and plunk it into our complex, multifarious, postmodern context. Without appropriation and transposition, it simply won't attend to the yearnings, needs, and circumstances of our day. Five hundred years is no small gap to be crossed.

Luther's context demanded that his theological lens be focused on the issue of grace and forgiveness. His revolutionary breakthrough was inextricably bound to the context of indulgences, the power of the pope, the relationship of the pope's power and domain to that of the Holy Roman emperor, and how God's will was perceived to be manifest in secular laws. But to tip the hand of following chapters, these factors are not ours. If we forget or ignore that fact, we do profound disservice to Luther, to those who read or hear him today, to the circumstances of our world, and to the way the gospel is stewarded in it. With that in mind, even though it's been done before, another review and perhaps reinterpretation of Luther is in order.

The Religious and Political Context of Luther's Day

As history would have it, Luther came onto the world stage when more than one scene was changing. The most obvious main characters in the plot of the Reformation moment are the church and the reigning (so to speak) politics of the day. It is nigh impossible to delve into the contextual import of the one without the other. In fact, references to both are found even in our creeds when we confess our faith in the one holy, catholic, and apostolic church.

> Luther came onto the world stage when more than one scene was changing.

Some Protestant worshippers cringe at, if not outright object to, the term *catholic*. "But we're not Catholic!" As it turns out, their fidelity to their faith tradition is appreciated but misplaced. The term *catholic* means universal and comes from the Greek *kata*, meaning *about*, and *holos*, meaning *whole*. When we recite the creeds, we are simply asserting that we believe that God is universal and that God is present across denominational lines.

However, in Luther's day, the Great (and complicated) Schism between the Western and the Eastern traditions notwithstanding, denominations per se were not yet a thing. In Western Europe at least, there really *was* one catholic church, the Roman Catholic Church. The church, however, held more than just ecclesial power; it was a political force as well and had been for over a thousand years. To understand the gravity and the import of this point, it's worth taking a quick step back for a long-lens historical view of the origins of what is now known as the relationship between church and state.

The Separation of Church and State

Until Constantine (272–337 CE) converted to Christianity, the Christian faith was illegal. And it wasn't just illegal; to be identified as a Christian was positively life-threatening. Christian adherents suffered not just persecution but martyrdom, and grisly martyrdom at that. For three hundred years, until Emperor Constantine came along, Christians lived a risky, tenuous existence because of their faith. Quite possibly thanks to his baptized mother, Constantine issued the Edict of Milan in 313, a decree that permitted the freedom of religious expression, including, notably, that of the Christian faith.

Although he was not formally baptized until just prior to his death in 337, Constantine evolved into the chief patron of the church. He built churches, encouraged and appointed religious leaders to political positions, and supported the church with massive donations of money and property. By way of setting the stage for the Reformation, Constantine's most relevant contribution was the creation of the Holy Roman Empire. Prior to Constantine, emperors understood themselves bound to honor and to be dutiful to the Roman gods; after Constantine's protection of and conversion to Christianity, their fidelity was transferred to faithful worship of the Triune, Christian God. With this singular move, the church, responsible for teaching proper dogma and ferreting out the unfaithful, could now turn to the state as the enforcer of the church's decrees. Heresy became not just a religious offense, but a secular one as well.

It was into this context, two decades after Constantine's death, that Augustine (354–430 CE) appeared. Augustine shaped the ensuing Christian tradition in countless ways, but for our purposes, his advent set the precedent for the modern definition of the roles of church and state.

Enter the Donatist controversy. The Donatists were a Christian splinter group that tried to act as a kind of purity police for the church. They asserted that anyone serving as clergy should have absolutely no history of apostasy or infidelity to God, and their lives must be faultless in order for their prayers and the sacraments to be valid. If not, their acts of ministry would be rendered blasphemous, therefore eternally to their condemnation and eternally worthless, as would the spiritual care received by the faithful to whom they ministered. Fully aware that a significant portion of the church's leadership and ministry was, by these standards, rendered null and void, the church declared the Donatists heretical. The church proper was particularly sensitive to the Donatists' objections, because several authorities had compromised their Christian identity under threat of persecution. The Donatists refused to submit to the leadership of these prior apostates. Their defiance irked the church leadership, but the offense was all the more compounded because the Donatists' stance spread, threatening precious ecclesial power. For this reason, a church commission under Constantine in 317 went further than just declaring the Donatists heretical; it declared the teaching of the Donatists anathema and illegal. In an attempt to unite the church, Constantine tempered his ire in 321, but the Donatists and Donatism remained a challenge to the church's authority and to that of the emperor.

The Donatists eventually declined, a turn that coincided with and was aided by Augustine's entry into the fray. Although some of Augustine's early writings supported religious liberty, reflection on the Donatist controversy changed his mind. He began to assert that the government had the authority to repress heretical groups either by forcing them into the strictures of the formal church or by punishing them by means of the state.

In 410, not long after the Donatist controversy settled down, the Germanic Visigoths sacked Rome. This terrible defeat of the city further cemented Augustine's take on the proper functioning of the roles of church and state. The invaders killed thousands of Roman citizens in the onslaught as they destroyed the entire city. In the wake of the attack, humbled and devastated, the people of Rome became convinced that their sufferings were palpable judgment by the Roman gods. They had abdicated Roman religious beliefs in favor of Christian ones and now were paying the price.

It was precisely this occasion that moved Augustine to write his famous *City of God*. In it, he sought to comfort and encourage the despondent Roman citizens and to assure them that their faith in the Christian God was still well placed. Regardless of whether Rome would pass away, the reign of God would not. Augustine employed the metaphor of two cities to make his point. One city, related to humankind, he called the Earthly City (referred to also as the Secular City, the City of the World, and the City of Man), and the other he called the City of God. Only God perceives who and what is in which city.

Because humanity is fundamentally sinful and base, Augustine said, our hearts and eyes must be kept trained on heaven—namely, on the Rule of God—and not trained on the distractions of earth and blinded by the rule of corrupt humanity. We are engaged in a battle between God and the devil, in which God, in an attempt to keep apostasy and sin at bay, established government and thereby order and a common moral ethic. Paradoxically, Augustine cautioned that government is itself a product of humanity (and therefore its depravity) and should itself be distrusted. Because it is created by God, one might assume that the church would, by default, find itself placed in the realm of the City of God. It's holy, after all. But no. Because Augustine was of the mind that the church, too, could be and was subject to sin and self-serving actions, it belonged in the Earthly City.

Pope Gelasius I (r. 492–496) disagreed, however. He felt quite firmly that not only did the church belong in the City of God, but in point of fact, as the representative of God on earth, all things, including the emperor, were subjected to the church's decrees. To that end, in 494, Gelasius crafted a letter to Emperor Anastasius entitled *Duo sunt* (meaning "there are two"). In it, he conceded that the church and political rulers had independent, critical yet distinct roles that complemented one another's tasks and roles in the reign of God. Also, and of key importance, because religious leaders had to provide a reckoning to God not only for their own faithfulness but also for those whom they encountered, political leaders were obviously subservient to the priests. Ultimate salvation trumped penultimate power, fundamentally flipping the hierarchy from the pre-Constantinian era. Moreover, Pope Gelasius claimed that the priests had the authority to dictate secular consequences for citizens who behaved unfaithfully. This nuanced separation of the powers, with the church now conveniently holding more influence, allowed for the subjugation of the state (granted, an anachronistic term) to the will of the church, and this delicate agreement enjoyed a full millennium of sway.

Popes who followed Gelasius largely enjoyed the benefits of the accepted truth that the church was to be viewed and trusted as if it simultaneously were and wielded the power of God. But over the centuries, this assertion of religio-political power began to annoy those in actual political power, ultimately festering into a tension that contributed to a long and complicated history between Rome and the secular rulers who reigned over the same lands as did the pope. It was this tension that benefited Luther and the Reformation he initiated on one fateful fall day in 1517. Luther had supporting actors waiting in the wings of the stage he didn't even know he was on.

A full millennium after Pope Gelasius's decree, the scene was beginning to shift. At the time of Luther, Germans were deeply committed to faith practices—on the surface. They worshipped holy relics, participated in the sacraments, and went on pilgrimages to holy sites. In many ways, religious devotion was at quite the fevered pitch. Simultaneously, the ever-present threat of wars, plagues, and crushing poverty was causing increased insecurity about the state of souls after death. Fear of death and damnation seemed to loom everywhere. Together, these factors fused to create deep anxiety and an eagerness for assurance from the religious leaders about one's eternal fate.

Simultaneously, a growing restlessness and even rebellion against the church were stirring within clerical and lay, political and civilian circles alike. The church's obsession with money and its questionable scruples helped drive this growing disgust, which ultimately blossomed into widespread disdain. For example, the papacy had a long history of extravagant living. In particular, Pope Leo X, who sat on the papal throne during a portion of Luther's tenure as monk, academic, and reformer, carried on this tradition with flair. Under Leo, Saint Peter's Basilica was being built in Rome, and to boot, the pope had quite an eye for fine works of art. These masterpieces didn't just magically appear on his walls and in his halls; instead, the costs to support such a lifestyle trickled down through the bishoprics of the church and through governing authorities who wanted to curry favor with church officials. Ultimately, of course, the laity got stuck with the hefty bill, disguised as an indulgence. It was these indulgences that directly sparked the smoldering components of the Reformation. The sale of indulgences created the piles of money that went south toward Rome to build Saint Peter's and fund the art habit of Pope Leo; ironically, indulgences created the crisis that threatened to undermine both.

Enter Luther

Martin Luther had no interest in, nor even a notion of, creating a new church. It was, after all, the *catholic* church, and he was a monk trained in the Augustinian Order of the church. He did, however, intend to reform it. To spur the necessary debate, Luther wrote Ninety-Five Theses, or statements, that legend has it were posted in public on the door of the Castle Church in Wittenberg in October 1517. The immediate motivation for Luther drawing up these assertions concerned the church's sale of indulgences, where people received, at a cost, either the remittance of their own sins or forgiveness of the sins of the soul of someone dearly departed.

> Martin Luther had no interest in, nor even a notion of, creating a new church.

Interestingly, Luther had no dispute with the pope's authority to issue the indulgences. Instead, he objected to them for at least three other reasons, all grounded in theological principles. First, repentance was reduced to a monetary transaction. Second, the fear of God was perceived as an opportunity to extort the poor. And finally, God's grace for us was dependent on our efforts.

Because his theses were geared toward the pope and academics for the purpose of debate, Luther wrote and posted them in Latin. Luther got his debate, and much more. Upon reading Luther's Ninety-Five Theses and other of his writings, in 1520, Pope Leo immediately issued a papal bull, an official document from the pope, called *Exsurge Domine* (Arise, O Lord). In it, he declared forty-one of Luther's theses heretical, and he demanded that Luther recant immediately. Luther's argument was primarily theological in nature, but the pope's reaction was driven by fiscal and political concerns: he realized that he was looking squarely in the eye of the potential loss of significant income and power.

For Luther, however, a burgeoning new understanding of the gospel was coming into his line of view, and it was this: the church was not necessary, per se, for salvation. Arguably, it potentially consternated faith in God, confusing it with faith in church. Not only did this subtle transfer of fidelity threaten first-commandment fidelity; it also encouraged trust in an institution that was more and more revealed to be corrupt. Given that threatening message (one that seemed to be catching on) exacerbated by the fact that he was accustomed to the past thousand years of religious and political authority, the pope was concerned by the implications of Luther's objections. In retrospect, however, he was hardly as aware of the existential threat to the ecclesial status quo as was his forefather Pope Gelasius when contending with the Donatists. The pope's initial reaction was neither as swift nor as firm as it could have been, because it seems as if he had not counted on this: Luther received widespread local and lay support for his cause. It was a level of support that took even Luther aback.

And how did this wildfire of support come to pass? The printing press stoked it, to be sure. Several printers published and widely distributed Luther's Ninety-Five Theses and his popular Sermon on Indulgences (written in German), making his theses available to a wide swath of German speakers and readers, as well as to academics. Luther's theological appeal cut across class and vocation: civilians (and also, therefore, laity) believed that in Luther, they had a hero for their various causes, and princes were glad that Luther appeared to have the power to finally weaken the pope's influence.

So a wave of support lifted Luther, ultimately catching the pope's attention. Albeit belatedly, the pope began to perceive more clearly the threat posed by Luther and therefore in 1520 issued his papal bull. It condemned Luther's teaching and threatened to excommunicate him unless he recanted. Although a later document (*Decet Romanum Pontificem*) officially excommunicated him, Luther's decision to call the pope the Antichrist and to burn *Exsurge Domine* essentially sealed that deal. Surprised but buoyed by the grassroots support for his ideas, Luther— never known for his diplomacy anyway—used his pen to continue the attack on the church and the pope. (Calling Pope Leo the Antichrist did not help foster a papal desire to stand down.)

Luther was officially excommunicated from the church in 1521. However, the pope decided this act alone was hardly sufficient to address Luther's numerous and severe infractions. He insisted that the new emperor, Charles V, impose civil punishment on him as well. This request put Charles in an annoying spot. Initially, Charles wanted little to do with this matter. In his new role as Holy Roman emperor, Charles had no interest in alienating the German princes and dukes, and he had any number of other crises commanding his attention. However, a diet— an assembly of the imperial states of the empire—was already scheduled to address different matters. It was to be held in the

German city of Worms, beginning in January 1521. The pope and various princes sympathetic to the established religious order persuaded Charles to command that Luther appear for trial before the diet.

Early on, Luther's principal ruler, Elector Frederick the Wise (1463–1525), served as Luther's self-appointed advocate. Frederick understood the stakes, both theological and political. So, because he had theological sympathies with Luther, and because Luther's cause was sympathetic with Frederick's own, the elector insisted that Luther be guaranteed safety both to and from the assembly. Charles V grudgingly agreed to the proposal, so with assurances of safety in hand, Luther arrived at the diet.

Per the new normal, the diet did not shape up as Luther had anticipated. He'd calibrated his expectations for a debate. Instead, awaiting him on a table were his writings and a question: "Are these your words?" Now, while much or all of this story is familiar, it is critical for our purposes to note something: at this point, Luther hesitated. Luther balked and then asked for time to think over his response; in fact, he did not return until the next day. It's an underplayed but crucial element of Luther's story arc and that of the Reformation: Luther experienced fear. As blustery as the man was, as renowned as he was for his insults and his wicked wit, despite having had the audacity to call the pope the Antichrist, Luther balked. Essentially, Luther told the assembled dignitaries, "I think I'd like to sleep on it. Give me a spell."

Why is it that Luther didn't simply own up to what was quite apparently true, namely, that these writings were clearly his and that he stood by them? It goes all the way back to Constantine and threads itself through Augustine and Gelasius. Luther knew that the pope had the long-steeped-in-history authority to excommunicate him as a heretic, but Charles V had the authority to kill him. Luther was not, therefore, being asked by a secular authority whether he wanted to recant. Rather, a secular authority imbued with power and an agenda from a religious authority was asking whether he wanted to live.

Clearly and demonstrably, Luther was hardly afraid of a verbal scuffle. In fact, he had already established that he relished a good fight if it were for the sake of the gospel. Fear of conflict, then, was not the reason for the pause. Fear for his life was. But here's the crucial point and the crucial moment: sometime between his request for time to reflect and his return to the chamber to announce his decision, Luther recalled that the church, the emperor, and even, therefore, death were just *penultimate.* He fell back on what had begun to bloom into not just a new way of understanding theology but a new way of understanding church: we are justified by nothing other than faith in the gospel. If we place our trust—trust that necessarily leads to our actions (our "works")—in anything other than the gospel, we have pledged allegiance to another god. We have broken the first commandment. We have focused on penultimate things.

Those gathered in that room to judge Luther knew that they had not just the secular authority to kill the body, but also the power to steal the courage of those seeking to live a life of faith. But Luther knew that he had something else: the gospel. It offered Luther confidence not in earthly institutions but in the cross and resurrection of Jesus. And so, Luther stood before the assembled dignitaries who cradled his fate, and he said this: "Unless I am convinced by the testimony of the Scriptures or by clear reason . . . I cannot and will not retract anything, since it is neither safe nor right to go against conscience." Although it is uncertain whether he actually said the following words, legend attests that Luther concluded, "I cannot do otherwise, here I stand, may God help me; amen."[1]

> Luther concluded, "I cannot do otherwise, here I stand, may God help me."

Given the stakes of the moment, Luther was motivated not by pride, ego, or bluster, but precisely this: faith in the crucified and risen Lord evoked in Luther revolutionary courage and freedom. The man spent the rest of his life trying to instill the very same in others.

That he had a life at all, post-diet, to use in spreading this gospel news is largely due to the friendly kidnapping and safe sanctuary organized by Frederick. For the better part of a year, Frederick concealed Luther in Wartburg Castle in Eisenach, a move that protected Luther from the bounty placed on his head following his appearance at the diet. Gratitude was perhaps not his primary response to this benevolent but forced imprisonment. Luther was not at all content being locked away in the castle tower. He grumbled somewhat petulantly about his "prison." Still, he chose not to languish, but instead crafted any number of letters and treatises. Perhaps most critically, it was during this time that Luther translated the New Testament into German, thereby also creating a unified, modern German language.

Meanwhile, although his physical presence was hidden, the effect of his writings was not. By 1522, in spite of the lack of Luther sightings, many fellow monks, townspeople, and political rulers had come to embrace Luther's views. As it played out, their faith in him turned to fervor, and the seeds of reformation grew into fast-growing tangles of revolution. The instability and even violence caused by his followers' ire toward the church compelled Luther to come out of hiding in order to be a voice— of all things—of moderation. Luther encouraged the people to recall his primary message: trust God and not earthly authorities. Earthly authorities can wield fear and punishment, but it is only our relationship to God that matters, and that should orient us to our ways in the world.

Now, for the purposes of this book, three impulses are relevant and must be teased out: Luther's understanding of the two kingdoms, Luther's belief in natural law, and Luther's view of justification. Each, in their own weighted way, informs both the standard interpretation and now a new interpretation of Luther's position about the Christian's calling to social justice.

The Two Kingdoms

To make his case all the clearer and all the more grounded, Luther began to develop his thought in the treatise *On Temporal Authority*, written in 1523. In this document and in a related but separate way in the 1519 *Two Kinds of Righteousness*, Luther sketched out his notion of the two kingdoms, a notion that not surprisingly sounded similar to Augustine's two cities in *The City of God*; he was, after all, an Augustinian monk.

With echoes of Augustine reverberating in his thought and in his personal recent history, Luther played out a dialectic between God's vision for humanity and the incapacity for humanity to carry it out. To make his case, Luther wrote of two kinds of righteousness. The first emanates from God, changing the sinner into someone justified—that is, someone righteous in God's eyes. The second sort of righteousness flows from the first. Because the righteousness of God inspires us to serve one another, we are by new nature and by faith placed into relationship with others. Cynthia Moe-Lobeda synthesizes Luther's insight this way: "Luther's understanding of justification is, thus, transformative. Justified sinners gradually are changed—individually but only in community—by the gratuitous righteousness of Christ." That is, all humanity is in need of redemption, and all humanity is, in a sense, contagiously redeemed by God's justification. Moe-Lobeda continues, "They are, in fact, 'made one with all others' by union with Christ."[2]

Additionally, Luther came to believe that God operates within two spheres, which he termed the Kingdom on the Right, and the Kingdom on the Left. In the Kingdom on the Right, God stirs up faith, right belief, and ways of being in the world that reflect one's Christian identity. Luther spoke of this status as humanity's standing before God (in Latin, *coram Deo*). The Kingdom on the Left, in contrast, is where Luther believed that human institutions, such as government, marriage, and *even the church*, land. Echoing Augustine, Luther said that because humanity is fundamentally inclined toward sin and self-preservation, laws and regular order need to be established. Without those, humanity would run free and therefore run wild. Luther referred to humanity's presence before others (that is, in relationship with the neighbor) as *coram hominibus*.

Both principles, *coram Deo* and *coram hominibus*, describe Luther's conviction that we are never only an individual; we are always in relationship to God and in relationship to others. It follows that we are always living, simultaneously, in both spheres. The goal, of course, is that we are calibrated to the Kingdom on the Right, so that even though we live in the Kingdom on the Left, we can more faithfully live out of the agenda of the Kingdom on the Right.[3]

Here we must circle back to this salient point: Luther quite intentionally stuck the church in the Kingdom on the Left. Like Augustine, he believed that church and governmental laws and structures are necessary. However, unlike Augustine, who believed the church was necessary because salvation outside of it was impossible, Luther believed the church was necessary because of humanity's inherent corruption. Insofar as each institution is created and run by humans, however, they are subject to the same inherent corruption and can lead people astray and cause them harm. This is no small matter.

Luther saw and experienced the corruption that often emerged when the distorted agendas of the Kingdoms on the Left and the Right meet. His unpleasant (euphemistically speaking) engagements with each bear powerfully upon our contemporary interpretation of Luther. Many descendants of Luther's Reformation misunderstand Luther's point here: Luther hoped to identify the nature and purpose of each kingdom, not (as is often believed) to create a strict wall between them. Recall that Luther placed the visible church in the Kingdom on the Left, right next to secular authorities.

To be sure, Luther understood that, theoretically and at best, the church is the arbiter of God's Word. It has a particular, noble, holy, vocational call to serve God and instill faithful belief in others. But Luther also understood— and experienced at Worms—that the church doesn't consistently fulfill its calling. The church, like individual believers, was *simul iustus et peccator*, both justified and sinful at the same time. But Luther didn't anchor his understanding of two kingdoms only in his views of humanity's depravity. Instead, the concept of natural law also fundamentally shaped his thinking.

> The church, like individual believers, was *simul iustus et peccator*, both justified and sinful at the same time.

Natural Law

The theory of natural law teaches that evidence of God's intention for the way things are is imprinted in nature. In other words, the apparently natural order, organization, and relationship of things are precisely as God planned and wants them. God's gift of reason to humanity allows us to discern God's will and ways.

Moreover, when we pay attention to the way things are (or seem to be), we notice not just (what seems to be) reality, but also God's unifying purposes. For example, natural law finds it no coincidence that parallels to the Ten Commandments appear in traditions outside of Judeo-Christianity.

However, natural-law theory poses some troubling questions of power and privilege. Those who get to declare things to be "normal" or natural and therefore God's will tend to be those with the authority, power, and privilege to define it as such. Political structures, Luther believed, are in place because natural law dictates that they be established as they are. But those who do not have authority or power have a fundamentally different experience of "normal." Oppression and inequity, they would say, should not ever be normal and are never God's will. But that thought does not seem to have crossed Luther's mind—nor, one could say, could it have. Natural law was an assumed truth. Turning to texts such as Romans 13 and 1 Peter 2, Luther made the case repeatedly and stridently that people of faith are to defer to civil authorities and established systems, including the likes of marriage, social strata, and the structures of the church. Possibly because observable patterns of social and political organization occurred long before Christ, he believed these established patterns of cultural and governmental structure that cut across eras and cultures are willed by God.[4]

Of course, Luther assumed that if all people were strict followers of Jesus, adherence to secular laws would not be necessary. But Luther knew that not all people are Christians, and he also knew that Christians are inherently sinful anyway.

Therefore, he believed that God created various forms of social ordering as an expression of God's love for us. Following them is a way of fidelity, serving God and serving the neighbor, whether Christian or not. Everyone needs secular (and natural) law to follow God's law. In fact, he believed Christians evangelize just by honoring established systems. Luther puts it this way: "The spiritual government or authority should direct the people vertically toward God that they may do right and be saved; just so the secular government should direct the people horizontally toward one another, seeing to it that body, property, honor, wife, child, house, home, and all manner of goods remain in peace and security and are blessed on earth. God wants the government of the world to be a symbol of true salvation and of His kingdom of heaven, like a pantomime or a mask."[5]

Like Augustine but unlike Gelasius, Luther believed that the church and the secular government are interrelated but distinct in role and purpose. He objected, then, when one began to assume the responsibilities of the other; in this way, the two structures were indeed separate. The papacy, therefore, had no business exercising or influencing the secular authorities, and in the same way, the secular government had no right to meddle in the affairs of the spiritual.

For this reason, Luther argued vehemently against those who sought to challenge and, worse, overthrow secular systems because of their religious beliefs. Such malcontents not only were confusing the roles of each institution, but also were disobeying secular, natural, and God-given laws. For this reason, Luther sided against the peasants during the Peasants' War.[6]

They were trying to shape worldly government on the basis of spiritual convictions. It should not be missed that these were the very spiritual convictions Luther himself awakened in the peasants. Luther believed that their revolt demonstrated an offense against God-given political authority and an overreach of their natural societal role. Luther's *Admonition to Peace* (1525) encouraged the princes to engage in a restrained approach to the peasants; it and his far more vitriolic tract *Against the Robbing and Murdering Hordes of Peasants* (1525) depend on and reveal his views on natural law.

Luther's reflections on the Sermon on the Mount also illustrate his views on the proper role of Christians who suffer injustice. Rather than engage in resistance, people of faith were to "turn the other cheek" and suffer in humility to God's natural law. In one representative passage, Luther declares:

> Christ teaches you . . . that you should still be willing to let everything be taken away from you, and do so gladly, doing good or contributing or lending where you can, and submitting to violence not only with regard to your property but also with regard to your life. . . . Especially should you be willing to do so for the sake of the Lord Christ, if you are threatened on account of the Gospel. . . . In other cases, involving secular affairs and the secular realm, you have the opportunity to appeal to judges and to the law if you have suffered injustice or violence, and to seek redress through them. But if you cannot secure justice or protection, then you have to suffer, just as even the non-Christians have to suffer.[7]

Ideally government was to be just, and citizens were to respect it as if it were. If the secular state were not ruling righteously, then objections could be faithfully raised. Still, at the end of the day, the decrees of government were to be obeyed.

We cannot interpret this text contextually, either calibrated to his time or ours, if we do not recall that Luther had absolutely no notion of democracy. The ability to have an opinion, wield it by way of a vote or a public protest, and expect that those in power would have the obligation to listen to and represent it was utterly foreign. Unlike today, when one can be a peanut farmer one decade and the president of the United States in another, people were born into stations that were immutable—though, it can well be argued, statistics indicate that for different reasons, perhaps times have not changed that significantly.

Repeatedly, then, Luther asserted that secular authorities be respected in secular matters, as they and their systems were providentially established by God. However, these same secular authorities were established *only* for secular purposes. When they presumed to speak for God in matters of the gospel, they trespassed their responsibilities and trampled on the spiritual well-being of their constituents.

> Luther asserted that secular authorities be respected in secular matters.

We see that distinction particularly laid out in Luther's treatise *On Temporal Authority*, not least of all in the following excerpt:

> For every kingdom must have its own laws and statutes; without law no kingdom or government can survive, as

everyday experience amply shows. The temporal government has laws which extend no further than to life and property and external affairs on earth, for God cannot and will not permit anyone but himself to rule over the soul. Therefore, where the temporal authority presumes to prescribe laws for the soul, it encroaches upon God's government and only misleads souls and destroys them.[8]

One more take on Luther's perspective on the separate powers of each "kingdom" is less theological and more practical. Lutheran theologian Deanna Thompson raises the question of whether Luther's viewpoints might have been motivated in no small measure by his awareness that he needed the state not only to prevent him from being killed but also to continue the wave of reform he had inadvertently, but with surprised satisfaction, initiated:

> We cannot get inside the mind of Luther, but we can appreciate the essential role princes played in his fight to shout down the fortress in Rome. Without temporal power on his side, Luther's words might have initiated uprisings, but dramatic reform would have come much more slowly. Luther did caution princes against abusing their power, for he could already sense that people would rise up if the princes refused to restrain their use of authority. At the same time, however, he implored Christians to accept temporal abuses of power as inevitable; in a fallen world, God's proper work could only act under the guise of God's alien work.[9]

That is, in Luther's mind, siding with the oppressed would have gone against not just God but his own self-interest, which by that time was quite invested in spreading his revolutionary theological and ecclesial views.

Indulgences and Justification

To reconsider the present Reformation moment, we must obviously also look at Luther's view on justification, which, of course, cannot be considered right and well without evaluating the role of the indulgence controversy first. As was earlier mentioned, indulgences served at least two purposes: they generated income necessary for building up Saint Peter's Basilica and the pope's art collection, and they also exploited people's sincere fears about their eternal salvation. The threat of death from disease, war, or simply the era's short life expectancy was everywhere. Terror about the afterlife was deep and pervasive. As one way of protecting themselves from God's wrath, people had become dependent on any number of rituals and practices that they believed—or at the very least, hoped—would stave off God's abandoning damnation. As necessary components to salvation, some combination of pilgrimages, relic worshipping, and self-flagellation was practiced routinely to appease the wrathful God.

These anxiety-driving activities did not go unnoticed by the church, which knew—as do modern-day marketers—that anxiety is a perfect emotion to exploit. The church needed funds and renewed loyalty, and the laity needed assurance about the status of their eternal life. Indulgences came to the rescue on both accounts. Curiously and conveniently, indulgences fostered the notion that no fundamental change—namely, repentance—was necessary for eternal salvation. A riff on Tetzel's famous jingle might be this: "As long as a coin in the coffer rings, I can keep doing all of these things!" In a very real and very base sense, the message was that God could be "bought off."

Interestingly, Luther's theological breakthrough about justification actually demanded more commitment from the people of faith ("the whole life of the believer should be penitence") than did the church. More interestingly, his message resonated and became a phenomenon. Clergy and laity alike felt resoundingly freed by the news that they had been declared righteous without eternally necessary self-promotional acts. Relief from anxiety, particularly while living in a social and ecclesial context where freedom from anything was at a premium, was exuberantly welcome.

Luther understood freedom, however, in a distinct and narrow religious context. Cynthia Moe-Lobeda sums up both the import and the impact of Luther's view of justification in this way:

> According to Luther, who we are because of Christ—first objects and then both objects and agents of God's love—determines also what freedom is. Freedom is, in the first place, freedom *from* "the foolish presumption that justification is acquired by works." That is, freedom is "from all works" as a means of purging away sins and attaining salvation. Freedom is, in the second place, *for* "trusting God" and *for* "giving myself as a Christ to my neighbor, just as Christ offered himself to me; I will do

nothing in this life except what I see is necessary, profitable, and salutary to my neighbor."[10]

Upshot: God's declaration that we are justified frees us from justifying ourselves in any way, whether justifying ourselves before God, justifying ourselves before others or justifying ourselves before ourselves. Assured of our righteousness in God's eyes, we are freed from fear, anxiety, and defensiveness. And assured of our own righteousness, we can be ambassadors of the same to others.

It is said that on occasion, preachers preach to themselves. In this case, it was surely so. Luther, who was himself afflicted with tendencies toward despair (*Anfechtung*), craved to hear that we are declared righteous and to experience this justification creating internal and external peace. This correlation mattered to Luther: justification, or "righteousness," must be established prior to peace, both scripturally and existentially. "But note," he wrote, "how the apostle places this spiritual peace only after righteousness has preceded it. For first he says, 'since we are justified (*iustificati*) by faith,' and then, 'we have peace' (Rom 5:1). Thus also in Ps 85:10, 'Righteousness and peace have kissed,' the term 'righteousness' precedes the word 'peace'. And again, 'In his days shall righteous flourish, and peace abound' (Ps 72:7)."[11]

His beloved Psalm 130 illustrates the same principle: "But there is forgiveness with you, so that you may be loved." Assured of God's promise of grace, we can fear *and* love God, rather than only fear God. This love for God is not to be hoarded but rather shared, and shared abundantly. Justification doesn't affect just one's individual relationship with God, but also one's individual relationship with the other. To this point, Moe-Lobeda turns to a 1526 text of Luther's treatise entitled *The Sacrament of the Body and Blood of Christ—against the Fanatics.* In it, Luther sketches out the link between justification and the extension of it. She writes, "Luther insists on the inseparability of [grace and extended love]: they are 'inscribed together as on a tablet which is always before our eyes and which we use daily.' . . . Justification by God is inseparable from a 'manner of life spent . . . in good works,' seeking the well-being of the neighbor without 'distinguish[ing] between friends and enemies.'"[12]

It may shock no small number of Lutherans to read here that Luther himself was not at all opposed to a "life spent in good works." Kindness and compassion to the other were, in his mind, a by-product of our own justification, our own experience of grace. Our active compassion toward the needy, Luther believed, occurs exactly because the grace offered to us is welcomed by our humility, that is, our recognition that none of us "deserves" grace. If grace were earned on the basis of merit, we would all fall short. Rather, receiving grace inspires grateful humility and good works toward other undeserving people.

> Luther himself was not at all opposed to a "life spent in good works."

Personal humility before God, that is, was not only an antidote of sorts to *Anfechtung*, but also an inspiration to relieve its presence in the lives of others. We see his view quite elegantly laid out in his reflection on the Magnificat, "My soul doth magnify the Lord, and my spirit hath rejoiced in God my Savior. For he hath regarded the low estate of his handmaiden" (Luke 1:46b–48a). Luther says, "Hence the stress lies not on the word 'low estate,' but on the word 'regarded.' For not her humility but God's regard is to be praised. When a prince takes a poor beggar by the hand, it is not the beggar's lowliness but the prince's grace and goodness that is to be commended. . . . [The] truly humble look not to the result of humility but with a simple heart regard things of low degree, and gladly associate with them."[13] That is, humble suffering is a mark of both God's presence and God's promise. Just as Jesus was crucified yet God overcame death exactly there, so too when we suffer not least of all for the sake of another, we can trust that God is at work stirring new life into being.

This message is clearly in keeping with Luther's theology of the cross. Although this theological theme is referenced only in his early works, its gist is this: God works in hidden ways, most particularly when out of death comes life. Luther's grasp of humility is, like all of his thought, grounded in his understanding of God. Rather than an experience of shame, humility is a radical openness to God's will and an act of extreme and total trust. Thompson writes:

> "Being humiliated" is a work God does to us rather than a work we do to ourselves. This act of God is none other than an attack on the sin residing within the sinful self. Far from indicating personal disengagement, Luther envisions passivity as a stance of total receptivity before

God, where personal will, private agendas, and desire no longer cloud one's relationship with God. Once the sinful gaze inward is shattered, Luther asserts, one's passive aptitude for a righteous spiritual life can be filled, through grace, with God's righteousness. Before others in society (*coram hominibus*), one then becomes utterly receptive to the needs and wounds of the neighbor. Spiritual humiliation, then, sets believers free for faithful living outwardly focused on *active* service to God.[14]

For any number of reasons, those of us with feminist sensibilities might be put off by words such as *humiliation* and *passivity*. But Thompson understands Luther to be teaching that people of faith stand before God completely open to God's agenda—an agenda that in turn empowers us to serve. Both terms, then, are defined by and oriented to God's agenda of service and liberation. Filled and imbued with God's righteousness, we become God's righteousness by way of compassion or prophetic work.[15]

I believe she is absolutely correct. Unfortunately, that's not how it has always worked out, and this is the crux, so to speak, of the matter facing us in this new Reformation moment.

Luther's notions of humility and his understanding of the two kingdoms and natural law have all too often fused in ways that further suppress and oppress people already suppressed and oppressed. In 1960, when still a graduate student in theology, Valerie Saiving Goldstein (1921–1992) wrote an essay that both affirms Luther's instincts and demonstrates their potential dire pitfalls. The groundbreaking essay is entitled "The Human

Situation: A Feminine View." In it, she acknowledges the prevailing theological assumption of the human situation—namely that humans are anxious—and maintains that sin drives us to seek to tamp down anxiety by "magnifying [humanity's] own power, righteousness, or knowledge. Man knows that he is merely a part of the whole, but he tries to convince himself and others that he *is* the whole. He tries, in fact, to become the whole."[16]

Theologians have long taught that this way of being in the world, this anxious compulsion that drives us toward self-centeredness, is our fundamental bent toward arrogant pride, which manifests itself in sinful acts. Fine, said Saiving, the theory works—if one is male. However, women have been taught to be precisely *not* proud. Rather, women are to be humble. The trouble is this: As an antidote, Christians have taught that love, defined by self-sacrifice, is the "precise opposite of sin." Just as pride is the source of all sin, tradition teaches us, self-giving love, also called humility, is the source of all goodness. Saiving made the case that while well intentioned, historically the theory hasn't played out well for women. I presume that sixty years hence, Saiving would have surely agreed that the same could be said for members of the LGBTQ+ community and people of color; their humility was—and too often still is—albeit in different ways, presumed, expected, and socially functional for the people with privilege and also power.

Tragically, people deprived of their full identities have often absorbed such suppressive messages and from them have even learned to overlook and disregard their self-worth. That is, the very thing that traditional theology has taught is most valuable—namely, selflessness—can be for women—and other oppressed groups—most detrimental. But for Luther and for centuries of theological reflection, this reframing of pride and humility would have been completely incomprehensible. People simply had divinely ordained stations in life. What we might consider now to be patently sexist, for example, was for Luther innately vocational, ordained by the laws of nature via God.

This moment is summoning us to reorient the definitions of justification, humility, pride, and call so that they reject the strictures of natural law and embrace an understanding of God that is bent toward liberation. Humility, as Luther defined it, was clearly about radical trust in God. But as it has played out, Luther's view of humility has also been a handy tool for suppression. It has enabled suffering by implying that suffering is a noble calling and even God's will. So we must now turn to Luther's theological and existential experience of suffering.

Suffering

Luther understood and experienced suffering in two primary ways. First, suffering results from defending the gospel against those who would seek to thwart or distort it. This perspective, in a nutshell, sums up his experiences from 1517 on, culminating at the Diet of Worms. Such persecution is due to faithfully living out of the Kingdom on the Right. Second, however, suffering takes place when people bear injustice that is, as he might have perceived it, *penultimate* suffering. Perhaps the oppressive circumstances are unfair, but the cause of people's suffering is due to the mores of natural law and the Kingdom on the Left. The gospel per se is not threatened, even if human beings and human rights are.

The Peasants' War, endured from 1524 to 1526, horrifically illustrates Luther's thinking on both accounts. The Reformation notwithstanding, the peasant population was already restless. The Black Death, which raced throughout Europe in the century preceding Luther, had killed about every other European citizen. As an unexpected consequence, the law of supply and demand tipped to more supply (that is, agricultural goods) than demand (people to eat them). Too much food meant cheaper food, which meant fewer coins in the pockets of the nobles.[17] Needing to find a way to compensate for their sudden lack of income, the landowners charged more rent to the peasants, increased the duration of the required leases, and even extended the contracts beyond the life of the tenant, thereby creating indentured servitude of the peasants' descendants. The church added to the demand for higher rent: to meet its increasing expenses in Rome, it taxed the princes, who in turn taxed the serfs. An inability to pay meant incarceration, which forced the free members of the family to work not only to pay back the debt, but also to pay the jailer for the release of the family member.

To be a peasant, then, was to despair of money, food, safety, and hope. To add insult to injury, peasants were aware that many of the lands they farmed were held by men with dual roles: they were princes and abbots of monasteries—men, that is, who represented God. In this context, Luther's words about justification and freedom touched the serfs and their lives of chronic suffering. He gave them reason to hope. He also gave them reason to revolt.

True though that is, it is crucial that we not import our understanding of revolt into Luther's day. The peasants were seeking fairness more than equality. One can even make the case that their demands were intended to reform and not completely dismantle the economic and social system. In 1525, just four years after Worms and two years after Luther's *On Temporal Authority*, the serfs wrote the "Twelve Articles of the Peasants," in which they asserted some theses of their own. This manifesto dipped into Scripture to make demands that were, by many accounts, entirely within the realm of reason: they wanted to choose their own pastors, requested that offerings stay within their parishes and not be sent off to Rome, sought fairer relationships between the workers and the landowners (even with the noted assurance that obedience to the nobles would be expected), hoped for reasonable expectations for work, asked for the establishment of fair rent, and so forth.

Like Luther, the peasants were so convinced of the basic integrity of their requests that they confidently and earnestly granted that if their articles were unsupportable by Scripture, they should be disregarded out of hand. If their demands were not consistent with the will of God, they would recant, so to speak. In this process, the peasants discovered the courage to assert the integrity of the experiences and their faith in the implications of the gospel. They simply wanted to align their grasp of their world with their grasp of the Word. Unfortunately, Luther did not at all anticipate these unintended social and political implications of his revolutionary theological thoughts. Ironically, the peasants "got it" better than did Luther. They could see that

Luther's theology liberated them from fear of God, fear of the church, and fear of being destined to live in squalor until Jesus came again. But that sort of consequence was news to Luther, and unwelcome news at that.

The peasants' misery was unethical and unjust, to be sure. However, Luther believed that the suffering of the peasants was not *because* of the gospel, but *for* the gospel. And here we see less Luther's understanding of the implications of the gospel and more his understanding of the implications of the two kingdoms and natural law: the established feudal system was in place because God intended it. The peasant uprising, therefore, threatened not only to break the peace, but also to break up a system that Luther believed God had intended. And if it threatened God, it therefore threatened the gospel. The threat had to be put down.

Worthy speculation adds this to the mix: Luther's vehement opposition had the side benefit of keeping the powerful on his side. Through the lens of politics and pragmatism, Luther knew that the peasants, poorly organized, funded, and trained, would be crushed by the powerful nobles. Those who offended the gospel and challenged his powerful allies could and should not win. And so, in his *Admonition to Peace* and later in his *Against the Murderous, Thieving Hordes of Peasants*, Luther condemned their cause. His words likely emboldened the nobles who waged war that led to the death of approximately 100,000 peasants.

The peasants and those sympathetic with them never forgot Luther's betrayal. His unwillingness to side with the peasants, not to mention his vile contribution to their suffering, affected not only the peasants of his day, but also those who have suffered because of systemic injustice since. His refusal to defend the sufferers, combined with his enabling of the system that suppressed them, has served as a role model, even if latent, for both quietists and for tyrants alike.

Reforming the Reformer

It's ironic that Lutherans have been reticent about challenging, about reforming, notions about Luther. One could argue that Lutherans have had a tendency to claim not only *sola fide* and *sola scriptura*, but also *solus Martinus Lutherus*! More than just *solus Lutherus*, we have tended to interpret Luther, and therefore the gospel, in one narrow way—namely, *sola gratia* (grace alone). Justification, that is, was not just the defining moment of the Reformation and not just the primary import of his theology for five hundred years, but also has been the primary—even the sole—way of understanding the essence of the gospel.

But the context—political, economic, social, and ecclesial—that created the perfect conditions for Luther's theological breakthrough is not ours. Moreover, it has not been for years and years. Fundamental elements of Luther's history must be reevaluated against the present context. First, Luther believed that we should resist authority but only when it concerns the gospel. As a case in point, Luther resisted the church's distortion of the gospel, one that took the form of indulgences, by writing the Ninety-Five Theses, and he resisted Charles V's distortion of political authority by refusing to renounce his writings. Both were perfect expressions of faithful resistance, for these authorities had injected themselves between the believer and God. Neither institution, said Luther, should be granted the authority that was due to only faith and Scripture. Understood in this sense, his *sola scriptura* and *sola fide* principles were important because they were not only claims of faith but also claims of courage.

> Fundamental elements of Luther's history must be reevaluated against the present context.

That said, he understood this dedicated allegiance to God very narrowly. While he opposed poverty, for example, he had no interest in overthrowing the very systems that generated the conditions for such poverty. Not only were those systems not interfering with people's direct faith relationship with God, they were themselves evidence of God's mysterious ways as manifested in natural law. When Luther referred to suffering that is worthy of protest, he understood it primarily as experiencing persecution because faith principles are threatened. In contrast, he saw "outward suffering" (e.g., hunger), even due to unjust systems, as something that one must bear. One's faith and one's standing before God are not in question, and Luther believed that secular laws, even those that could cause unjust suffering, are themselves expressions of God's occasionally mysterious ordering of society.

It's interesting that Luther wrote *On Temporal Authority* just two years after having a bounty placed on his head. Recall that the pope could excommunicate but the emperor could kill.

No wonder, then, that immediately after he found himself in the crosshairs of the overlapping powers of church and government, Luther wrote *On Temporal Authority* and then later the Marburg treatise on the *Two Forms of Righteousness*. In other words, post-Worms, Luther was quite keen on establishing the proper roles of both institutions, not least of all because his very life had been threatened by each when leaders misappropriated power. His vocation was therefore spent calling out their respective unacceptable authority over people's relationship with God.

As was the prevailing view, Luther had no doubt that natural law decrees that because things are as they are, they are as God intends them to be. Revolting against governmental policy, therefore, revolts against God. When gospel—namely, the right relationship between God and the believer—is not at issue, a person of faith should simply bear the political and social circumstances, no matter how dire. As long as the person of faith trusts that salvatory matters between the believer and God are in order, all is in order.

One *can* make the case that Luther's outrage about indulgences was, in part, driven by economic outrage at the implicit extortion afoot, but Luther's primary objection was that of distorted grace. Economic exploitation was a secondary, not primary, affront. But if gospel is *soteria*—namely, health, healing, and wholeness (and not merely that Jesus forgives sins)—then wherever the *soteria* gospel is threatened, in church or in government, we are justified and freed to courageously protest, resist, defend, and even upheave.

This is the nexus of the new Reformation of our moment: per Luther, the gospel includes the declaration of justification, but it extends its essence to the summons to justice, for where there is injustice, then health, healing, and wholeness—*life*—are all threatened. We are followers of Jesus, and therefore ambassadors of his gospel, which proclaims that death is real, but life is realer.

In the name of the risen Christ and in accord with his agenda, we are here to announce, protect, and enact it.

Discussion Questions

1. According to the author, what circumstances in Luther's context demanded that his theological lens be focused on the issue of grace and forgiveness?

2. How does the author talk about the relationship between church and state, both historically and theologically? How did this relationship affect Luther in his day? In general, how is this relationship defined in our own society today?

3. Luther's understanding of the world as he saw it included three important perspectives: his views of the two kingdoms, natural law, and justification. The author unpacks each of these topics in a detailed way. How are Luther's views on these topics described?

4. As an example, the author speaks of the Peasants' Revolt. How did Luther's views of two kingdoms and natural law seem to affect the tragic outcome of the

revolt? How might Luther's views of these topics also lead to the oppression or suppression of certain people even in our day?

5. Reread this sentence: "But if gospel is *soteria*—namely, health, healing, and wholeness (and not merely that Jesus forgives sins)—then wherever the *soteria* gospel is threatened, in church or in government, we are justified and freed to courageously protest, resist, defend, and even upheave." What is your response to that idea?

4

Here They Stood

Luther's theological well is wide and deep. For over five hundred years, Lutherans and Christians across the spectrum have dipped heavily into it, finding there God and grace. By no means is it time to put a lid on that well, for the water is still sweet and fresh and abundant. However, it is time to haul that water to the context of today's global, interdependent world, where people will be satisfied by it for new and different reasons.

For five centuries, we have lifted Luther's words and convictions from his time into the contemporary one, doing so out of grand gratitude and respect for him and his fundamental reframing of grace and gospel. His rediscovery of *sola gratia* has provided relief and hope to countless faithful—and unfaithful!—people. However, understated and overlooked elements of his theology, along with assumptions about it, have pointedly missed evangelical opportunities and have even done great harm. We are seeing some of the effects of that reality today.

Sometimes we simply forget that circumstances were different back in Luther's day. We easily forget, for example, that although Luther and his immediate world were well aware of people beyond their immediate community (they were fighting with Rome, after all, and were becoming increasingly aware of the threat of the Ottoman Empire), they were only beginning to learn how much more expansive the world was than their imaginations had before considered. Recall that Luther was a young boy when Columbus made his world-changing venture across the sea—one, of course, that less "discovered" a new land than led to the decimation of numerous cultures and peoples.

We easily forget that although Luther and his immediate world trusted in natural law as a natural assumption, they had no concept of the inherent inequity and power roles it fosters.

We easily forget that Luther and his immediate world knew of a political system that was hierarchical and determined by birth. It wasn't until more than two hundred years after his death that the construct of democracy as we are familiar with it in the United States was introduced.

We easily forget that Luther and his immediate world knew of gender roles. These roles had even begun to be slightly stretched (in part due to Luther himself, even if moderately by our standards). However, movements called "women's rights," "women's right to choose," and the possibility of women's ordination were not at all on the collective radar.

We easily forget that Luther and his world knew of non-Christians and interacted with those who professed faith differently—Judaism and Islam, in particular. But they knew very little of widespread cultural atheism, agnosticism, or the Nones (those with no religious affiliation).

We must not forget, for example, that Luther and his immediate world knew positively nothing of Black Lives Matter, March for Our Lives, LGBTQ+ rights, postmodernism, feminism, womanism, Dalit theology, liberation theology, the labor movement, fears of global warming and climate change, and plastic bottles choking the seas. Nor did he know of the Holocaust, 9/11, and white nationalists. The cultural, social, economic, political, and ecclesiastical differences between Luther's world and ours aren't just intriguing to note; they have profound, wildly underrecognized theological implications.

For several decades, theologians from across continents and perspectives have been noticing that Luther's emphasis on justification, while right and deeply valuable, no longer suffices as the sole or even the primary point of the gospel. No one is opposed to forgiveness, of course! The gospel, though, must have something to say not just to the sinners, but also to those sinned against. It must have something to say not just to sinful individuals but also to sinful systems. Without this corrective, Luther's theological breakthrough becomes a theological barrier erected between the sinners and those sinned upon, and between the empowered and the powerless.

By expanding and reinterpreting Luther's notion of justification so that it includes or is included by notions of justice, we not only engage in our own new reformation of the gospel, but we also can be better ambassadors of it in new and salvatory ways now. To begin our reframing of the gospel, it is well to bend our ears toward people who have suffered injustice and grief.

When my daughter was five, she said to me, "Mama, I've been thinking about parenting lately."

I paused. "Really, sweet thing? Tell me, baby girl, tell me what you have been thinking about parenting."

> To begin our reframing of the gospel, it is well to bend our ears toward people who have suffered injustice and grief.

"Well, it's dawned on me that when you have children, it's like you move to a different country. You can go back and visit your other country, the one where your friends who don't have kids live, but you can't live there anymore, because you have children now and they don't. And they can come and visit you in your new country, but they can't live there until they have children."

She was absolutely right, of course. It's simply true that having children profoundly affects one's life experience, mores, traditions, and routines. It isn't about better or worse, but it is about a distinctly different reality. And while she was right about that, the very same thing can be said about suffering. When you have suffered, everything changes. You become profoundly different. You may have a "work visa" of sorts that allows you to mill about in your former world, but your new world belongs to a different place where normal is different, where language is different, where habits are different, and where perceptions ot what is real and true and important are different. The people and trends I review below live or lived in a different country and time than did Luther. They drink from Luther's well of free and abundant grace, but they serve it up in various countries, literally and figuratively, where suffering of various sorts is the history and, in varying degrees and ways, still the active norm.

Jesus

Joe Hill (1879–1915) was a Swedish immigrant who worked as an itinerant laborer. His was a harsh life, filled with daily threats to safety, health, and fair compensation for work. Thinking that unions could improve the workers' lot, Hill joined the Industrial Workers of the World (aka the Wobblies) and became a songwriter and cartoonist for their cause. It was he who came up with the well-known phrase "pie in the sky by and by," which surfaced in his spoof of the beloved gospel tune "The Sweet By and By," written in 1868 by Sanford F. Bennett (1836–1898) and Joseph Webster (1819–1875) and still a golden oldie in the gospel and country music scene. Their song's cadence and lyrics made it an immediate classic:

> There's a land that is fairer than day,
> And by faith we can see it afar;
> For the Father waits over the way
> To prepare us a dwelling place there.
>
> *Refrain*
> In the sweet by and by,

We shall meet on that beautiful shore;
In the sweet by and by,
We shall meet on that beautiful shore.

We shall sing on that beautiful shore
The melodious songs of the blessed;
And our spirits shall sorrow no more,
Not a sigh for the blessing of rest.

Joe Hill positively hated this hymn (Mark Twain was no fan of the song either). Hill knew full-well that destitute workers suffered desperate conditions daily; they didn't need relief later in some sweet by and by. They craved and clamored for it now. So in 1911, Hill took a pen in hand and wrote his retort, the parody he titled "The Preacher and the Slave":

Long-haired preachers come out every night
Try to tell you what's wrong and what's right
But when asked how 'bout something to eat
They will answer in voices so sweet:
You will eat, bye and bye
You will eat, bye and bye
In that glorious land above the sky
Work and pray, live on hay
You'll get pie in the sky when you die.

In short, Hill didn't want pie later. He and those for whom he spoke wanted pie today. A Jesus who didn't intervene with practical, tangible salvation in the now was as useless and mockable as were the people who represented him.

It's a safe bet that Hill didn't realize it at the time, but he was engaging in a debate about Christology, namely, the study of the role, identity, and effect of Jesus Christ. Christology raises all sorts of questions, but most relevant to the task at hand is this one: Can we experience or work to bring about the tangible, saving presence of the reign of Jesus now, or are we instead meant to be satisfied and edified by hope that one day, after we die, we will find God's foretold peace?

Of course, Luther believed and taught that Christians are to be active in kindness toward others; he called us to be "little Christs," after all.[1] We help the poor, we feed the hungry, we offer compassion to the troubled, and we comfort the grieving. But Luther had little inclination for Christians, in the name of Christ, to call out and work to overturn the basic systems that *create* human suffering. His encouragement to those who were subject to political and social structures that perpetuate suffering was, essentially, that they should wait for the strudel by and by.

> Can we experience or work to bring about the tangible, saving presence of the reign of Jesus now?

"The Sweet By and By" emphasizes hope for the future and tolerance for the present. "The Preacher and the Slave" raises a voice for resistance in the present and really has very little interest in any post-death future. Theologies that help us transpose Luther's thought into the key of today would like to adapt the best of both tunes: hope for the future, but not such that we are blinded to the systemic injustice and pain that many suffer in the present.

In essence, these voices are looking to reappraise, reappropriate, and repurpose Luther's understanding of the first commandment. In his *Large Catechism*, Luther sketched his takeaway of God's first commandment in this way:

> This much, however, should be said to the common people, so that they may mark well and remember the sense of this commandment: we are to trust in God alone, to look to him alone, and to expect him to give us only good things; for it is God who gives us body, life, food, drink, nourishment, health, protection, peace, and all necessary temporal and eternal blessings. In addition, God protects us from misfortune and rescues and delivers us when any evil befalls us. It is God alone . . . from whom we receive everything good and by whom we are delivered from all evil.[2]

To those who place their ultimate faith in saints, sorcery, silver, astrology, their social station, and personal skill (just a few examples of apostasy Luther also listed in his explanation), Luther rails that "the trouble is that their trust is false and wrong; for it is not placed in the one God, apart from whom there truly is no God in heaven or upon earth."[3] In contrast, says Luther, those who instead place their faith solely in God are filled with integrity, fidelity, and true hope, for they know to worship one worthy of their trust. God can be trusted because God is ultimately merciful.

Now, in chapter 1 of this book, Luther's definition of God, based on his understanding of the first commandment, established a framework we can use for thinking about our new Reformation moment. Right now, that is, I believe that individually and communally we are being asked whether God is, in fact, our God. Any number of alternate gods are requesting, if not demanding, our allegiance. Given that, Luther's interpretation of the first commandment is not just enduringly helpful, but enduringly essential: the true God, rather than false gods, deserves our trust.

However, Luther's reflections express some problematic assumptions about God and life that, frankly, are not necessarily true. For example, people do not always have food, drink, nourishment, health, protection, and peace. To attribute trust and thanks to God for that which is in fact all too often painfully absent ranges from insensitive to cruel. Ironically, the explanation of the first commandment could undercut faith in the God to which the first commandment points! Those who suffer now need relief now (cue Joe Hill). Obviously, when one is starving, hurting, hiding in fear, or grieving, promises of God's eternal mercy offer hope. This is good! But such hope would not be needed in the same desperate key were people to be presently and actually satiated, healed, safe, and comforted. Then hope in mercy would have been transformed into actual, merciful, tangible *soteria* (salvation): health, healing, and wholeness.

Christians have responded to the first-commandment question about who God is by pointing to Jesus—not that that calls the matter a wrap! Christology, this study of who Jesus is, is complex and sometimes contentious, yet it is always fascinating from both a historical standpoint and a perspective of consequence. Who we think Jesus was and what he means affect who we think we are to be and what we are to do. Often, the study of Jesus has been divided into two approaches: Christology from above and Christology from below. Much of white, Western, and therefore predominant theology has depended on a Christology from above, yet traditions that depend more on a perspective stemming out of a Christology from below have words of wisdom that need to be heard now and have needed to be heard for a long, long time. To them we now turn.

Christology

Volumes have been written about the two christological points of view, but for our purposes, this simple distinction will do: Those who gravitate toward a Christology from above are drawn to theologies that start by way of theories about God. These theories, hunches, and convictions about God are gleaned through various forms of revelation as found in Scripture, nature, mystical experiences, and academic reflection. Theologies that come out of a Christology from above are particularly curious about the divinity of God. A Christology from above finds its scriptural home in the Gospel of John and the notion of a preexisting *Logo*s, the Word that has always existed. Some readers may be familiar with the hymn "When Long before Time," which is a fine adaptation of the best of Christology-from-above theology.

In contrast, a Christology from below is far more interested in the human Jesus, his ministry, and his sufferings while he lived. Theologians who gravitate to this christological model look not only to the Synoptic Gospels (Matthew, Mark, and Luke) and Acts for their scriptural anchors, but also to accessible experiences of suffering as valid occasions of revelation and experience of God's active presence. For example, the late African American systematic theologian James Cone (1938–2018) dedicated his life to studying theology from the perspective of the black experience in the United States, therefore as a theologian "from below." His insights serve as both a critique and a clarification of Luther's view of the first commandment. Cone viewed everything theologically through the lens of the systemic manner by which black lives have been devalued in America and its history. In their pain, he saw—and wants us to see—Jesus: his sufferings, his protest, and his solidarity with those who suffer and grieve.

This persistent reality began for blacks when they were stolen from their native lands and then were seen as mere chattel, as property to be used for the sake of white power and privilege. However, in contrast to livestock, the enslaved people presented a constant threat of rebellion and revolt. That fear alone compelled white owners to bring those they had enslaved to church, if for no other reason than to prevent them from organizing when the masters were away at worship. In addition, though, the owners felt an obligation to "evangelize" the enslaved people. It turns out, said Cone, that when black enslaved persons were forced to listen to the white Jesus, they heard something that the white worshippers didn't. Precisely their searing experience as

enslaved people helped them detect the promise of liberation—
of liberation such as the people of Israel actually experienced in
the exodus. They picked up that the gospel is not about oppression, violence, fear, or contented comfort in the pews. It is about
incarnate hope.

Ultimately, their lives of suffering and their hard-earned
hearkening to the Word led to a theological break with the white
church tradition. Cone describes it this way:

> We black theologians had to ask what the gospel has to
> do with life and death and the struggle of people to be
> free in an extreme situation of oppression. The existen-
> tial and political implications of this question forced us
> to take a new look at the theological enterprise, and we
> concluded that the beginning and the end of the Chris-
> tian faith is found in the struggle for justice on behalf
> of the victims of oppressive societal structures. What-
> ever else Christian theology might be, it must take sides
> with the victims who are economically and politically
> oppressed. If theology does not side with the victims of
> economic injustice, it cannot represent the Victim Jesus
> of Nazareth, who was crucified because he was a threat
> to the political and religious structures of his time.[4]

Straight out of the chute here, Cone says that in the face of
the particular experience of chronic racism, black Christians
needed "to ask what the gospel has to do with life and death and
the struggle of people to be free in an extreme situation of

oppression." It's a stunning statement that has nothing to do with pie to be enjoyed at some later, post-death, heavenly church social. Instead, black Christians asked what difference the gospel makes *in the midst* of suffering, inclusive of but beyond eschatological hope. Instead, it became of tantamount importance and terrible consequence that "the Victim Jesus of Nazareth" was crucified "because he was a threat to the political and religious structures of his time." This tradition cherished the truth that in his lifetime, Jesus didn't just offer *eventual* hope and help. Rather, he engaged the unjust power structures and systems, and he did so to such a degree that the threatened authorities had to kill him. That experienced truth of Jesus resonated with those who themselves suffered unjustly and resisted. It also inspired the conviction that any Christian theology that falls short of this same commitment to "take sides with the victims" falls short of both terms, *Christian* and *theology*.

Of course, Cone was implicating the predominant white theological tradition, one traditionally far more comfortable with theological theories than theological praxis. In fact, the tendency to placidly *theorize about* rather than *actively engage* oppressive powers has led whites to create a God who professor of Christian Ethics Reggie Williams provocatively says

> Christian theology that falls short of this same commitment to "take sides with the victims" falls short of both terms, *Christian* and *theology*.

"could be described as sadistic; he was a transcendent peda-gogue who stood at a distance, coming near only to chastise the sinner with misery."[5]

Even Dietrich Bonhoeffer (1906–1945), a white theologian and Christian who ultimately received true props from Cone, primarily knew *that* God. Or he did until he experienced black Harlem during his time at Union Seminary in the 1930s. There Bonhoeffer was struck vocationally, theologically, and existen-tially, not by Union Seminary, which taught more or less famil-iar white, ivory-towered theology (he'd had his fair share and more of that in Germany), but by black hymnody. These spiritu-als focused on Jesus's "solidarity with social outcasts, even unto death. That explains why the lived experience of Jesus' cross for black people in America was one of the most often repeated themes within the spirituals, as evidenced by the question in the spiritual 'Were You There?'"[6]

Traditional black theology, in contrast to the habits of tra-ditional white theology, sees present suffering echoed in Jesus's past suffering and, in turn, the suffering of Jesus present in current pain and grief. Jesus's sufferings are our sufferings, and our sufferings—individual and collective—are Jesus's. The hymn, with its haunting tune and lines, "Were you there when they crucified my Lord . . . nailed him to the tree . . . laid him in the tomb?" places the singer right there with Jesus's trauma. When the spiritual is sung, one doesn't sing *about* Jesus; one sings *with* Jesus. Black theology simply embraces the truth that Jesus's life, death, and resurrection affect life and the choices in it in every moment.

Bonhoeffer was powerfully shaped by this transposition of Jesus's suffering solidarity into present suffering. Jesus is in all of us, and we are all in Jesus. The influence of this theology can be found in any number of Bonhoeffer's writings, including *The Cost of Discipleship*. As but one example, he writes:

> [The New Testament] holds that the church community claims a physical space here on earth not only for its worship and its order, but also for the daily life of its members. That is why we must now speak of the *living space* [*Lebensraum*] of the visible church community.
>
> Jesus' community with his disciples was all-encompassing, extending to all areas of life. The individual's entire life was lived within this community of the disciples. And this community is a living witness to the bodily humanity of the Son of God. The bodily presence of the Son of God demands the bodily commitment to him and with him throughout one's daily life. With all our bodily living, existence, we belong to him who took on a human body for our sake. In following him, the disciple is inseparably linked to the body of Jesus.[7]

Black theology echoes throughout these words, keen as it is to trust that God intends to bring salvation to the fore *now*, which is not least of all a repudiation of natural law, a core component of Luther's theology. In fact, as was the case for the peasants in Luther's day, so too has it been and too often continues to be for black people; their oppression has been tolerated as normal and inevitable. Williams only has to point to the culturally accepted "pejorative images of indolent, lawless, licentious black people," which became such an embedded perception of African Americans that "suffering [became] a natural, inevitable, even theologically appropriate part of black life."[8] The nexus of natural law and of notions of a God whose primary role is to offer hope in the meantime rather than help in the moment has enabled and even condoned racial suffering, as well as the perpetuation and the toleration of systemic sin.

While not uniquely, African Americans have suffered much under the presumptive underpinnings and effects of natural law. Their experience illustrates the way in which privileged theology begets quietude, prejudice, suffering, and the toleration of the oppressive status quo. In contrast, the gospel, with its promise of *soteria*—health, healing, and wholeness—repudiates applications of natural law when it condones and perpetuates racism and any other system of oppression.

Sin

Luther defined sin as misdirected trust. It's an obvious corollary to his definition of God: God is that in which or in whom we place our ultimate trust. Thus, if we trust in something that is not *God*, we are trusting in a *god*, which is sinful. Anytime we act in a way that displays lack of fidelity to God and place our trust instead in a god, we sin.

Because Luther's immediate context was concerned about ways to be freed of individual sin (one's own or that of loved ones who had died), Luther obviously focused on the relief for individual sin. Without question, Luther expressed and extended concern for the neighbor, but it is crucial to note that his primary agenda was the reformation of the church's teaching about sin and forgiveness. Therefore, his focus of concern was to emphasize grace offered to the individual. Nothing, including the church and secular powers, could affect whether or not a person would be declared righteous, for that declaration was God's alone. The church was not necessary, money was not necessary, good works were not necessary for grace. One's relationship to God through faith was the only key.

Unfortunately, this focus on individual sin and the freedom of forgiveness has been set on auto-repeat throughout consequent ages. Effectively, this singular emphasis on personal sin (itself an ironic manifestation of *in curvatus se*) allowed for many people of faith to notice little, if any, relevance or application of the gospel to a broader, systemic, justice-focused notion of sin. That is, the prevailing theological traditions appreciated that a *person* is sinful and in need of repentance. But that *people*, organized as a family, as a congregation, as a business, as a political system, as a culture, are systems also in need of repentance—that has received relatively less play.

It is a severely underrepresented truth that individual sin causes collective, collateral, and individual suffering. As theologian Cynthia Moe-Lobeda says, "Collectively, we are selves curved in on ourselves. We may long to live according to justice-making, self-honoring love for Earth and neighbor, to live without exploiting neighbor or Earth. But look at us. A species destroying the very life-support systems upon which life depends.

A society so addicted to our consumption-oriented ways that we close our hearts and minds to the death and destruction required to sustain them."[9]

Denominations such as the Evangelical Lutheran Church in America, the Episcopal Church, the United Church of Christ, and the Presbyterians (to list but a few) have crafted powerful, pointed, and pastoral social statements addressing racism, violence, creation care, health care, abortion, and economic justice. These statements are richly rooted in Scripture and in savvy awareness of the complexities of the day. These denominations have experienced no small or insignificant pushback for their boldness. It is all the more pronounced at the congregational level. Within a parish, naming individual sin, albeit in a blanket fashion, is allowed and expected. People have a sense of the expected parameters of what is and is not appropriate Christian living. But things get dicier when one begins to call out not just racism writ large, but specific racist behaviors and policies; not just poverty, but capitalism's creation and fostering of it; not just prayers for the sick, but prayers for health insurance for all; not just the care of creation, but the reduction of fossil fuels and single-use plastics. It's awfully risky and understandably scary to name communal sin as boldly as one calls out individual sin.

We might seek to navigate those waters by sincerely advocating that people bring cans for the hungry or donate to a homeless shelter. Perhaps that will suffice, we hope. But Moe-Lobeda frames the slipperiness of sin this way: "If I am professing love for neighbor by feeding the poor and sheltering the homeless, and yet am ignoring the systemic factors that have made them hungry and homeless, am I loving neighbor?" Instead, it is the very dismantling of those systemic factors that express and embody radical neighborly love.[10] That sort of provocative faith ethic has no patience for natural law or pie in the sky by and by. It sees what many would prefer not to see—namely, that what often passes as benevolent donations such as these actually enables the oppressive systems to continue. The somewhat tired analogy of the people falling into the river may apply here: Do you keep pulling people out of the river who only go back to the top to fall in again, or do you stop them from falling in in the first place? Feeding the hungry pulls them temporarily out of poverty; creating a fair economic system stops them from falling into poverty in the first place.

This new Reformation moment calls for us to stop the drownings by damming the river access. Luther, of course, was quite comfortable giving alms (pulling people out of the river), but overturning political and social and economic systems (damming it)? As far as he saw, this tactic not only *did not represent* the gospel, it was *antithetical* to the gospel. The unconditional reconciliation of the private sinner to God was the essence of the gospel; anything else was a distraction, if not a temptation, from it.

> Feeding the hungry pulls them temporarily out of poverty; creating a fair economic system stops them from falling into poverty in the first place.

With this in mind, then, the fundamental restructuring of society as a mode of faith is a tough sell to those whose beliefs stem from Luther's heritage. It is preferable and more comfortable to speak of cultural, social, political *reconciliation*; this is an easier pitch, not least of all because it dovetails nicely with familiar Lutheran notions of forgiveness.

But voices are rising that question whether the quick move to reconciliation might be actually a quick retreat from accountability and, in a word, reformation. One such voice is Erna Kim Hackett, the associate national director of urban programs for InterVarsity and a woman of Korean and Caucasian background. Hackett has significant apprehensions about the ease and speed with which people of privilege speak of reconciliation. The second portion of the word *reconcile* comes from *concilare*, which means to be friendly. That, coupled with the *re* prefix, meaning again, spells trouble for her: "be friendly again" is what the word means. But, she asks, "when have white people ever been in just relationship with black people? During slavery? During Jim Crow? During the War on Drugs? What are we RE-conciling? It pretends that there was a time when everything was fine, we just need to get back there. However, that idyllic time has never existed."[11]

Hackett sees clearly what privileged people see dimly, if at all. There is a culture of injustice, and privileged people are complicit in it and reap benefits from it. Moreover, if this is true, the gospel must mean something more than reconciliation, than forgiveness. In fact, it may even compel a fundamental reevaluation of reality, one that might transform everything, even the long-trusted faith language and tenets.

Movie buffs can find an analogy in *The Matrix*, perhaps most particularly in the deeply jarring scene in which Neo is extricated from artificial reality into true reality. He had been living in an illusion that he and the world had believed to be real, but that in fact was untrue. The removal from the lie is wrenching, painful, and brutal. But after it, Neo sees revealed reality, and for the first time, he is free. The cross works in this way, too. The promise that death does not win frees us from protecting our lives, our privilege, and our illusions, and it frees us to see reality for what it is: everything and everyone is God's and is loved. Repenting of our self-invested privilege, instead of reconciling ourselves with those whom our privilege has exploited and dismissed, establishes the possibility for relationships rooted in the notion of redemption. In Christ, salvation—health, healing, and wholeness—has come to these relationships to reappraise, redefine, and renew them.

Confronting personal and collective sin is fiendishly difficult to do because in doing so, we are, in fact, sacrificing our lives—or at least our way of life. The process is all the more complicated because, in an effort to preserve ourselves, we distrust our impression of what is being seen. Some years ago, I read a book on narcissism by Sandy Hotchkiss. While the entire book is worth the read, especially for those who have experienced difficulties and abuse because of contact or relationship with a narcissist, arguably the most helpful line in the book was this:

We all view life through the lens of these experiences, but the Narcissist has something more, not just a lens but a prism that refracts and distorts incoming messages to avoid the intolerable feeling of shame. This means that you are never in control of how these people perceive you, or when you will be assaulted with some defensive maneuver that deflects their shame, prevents their deflation, or reinflates them after narcissistic injury.[12]

Narcissists, you see, distort the issue for their own self-protection. We aren't all narcissists, of course. But we can see a societal tendency to adapt and adopt elements of narcissistic behavior: frequent attempts, not least of all, to redefine the issue in a way that absolves one of responsibility for fundamental change. The *other* is to make the changes to make the system work. Cynthia Moe-Lobeda calls one's perspective on reality his or her "moral vision." The term, however, encompasses moral and immoral visions. To preserve our lives, we peer through a prism of privilege and see collective, chronic, systemic, and immoral actions as "good."

Much like the narcissist, then, the broad community can distort reality to protect its own interests, self-perception, and way of life. Moe-Lobeda writes, "Vision is constructed to normalize and rationalize existing social and ecological conditions (the way things are) that may be evil, allowing them to parade as good, inevitable, or normal. This entails *not* seeing (or seeing but disregarding) evidence to the contrary."[13] This is exactly the M.O. of a narcissist, and the M.O. of much of predominant culture, society, and policy-making.

Within our Lutheran tradition, we have resources within Luther's own work to come to our rescue here: he spoke not about seeing a thing as it is, but about calling a thing what it is. Those are words that call for prophetic speech and for prophetic action based on prophetic speech.

Systemic and Personal Suffering

Systemic sin uses many tools to maintain its power. Intimidation and even fear are some of the most dastardly and effective resources available to keep an oppressive system going. They were, in fact, precisely Luther's experience at Worms. He was afraid—not least of all afraid for his life—and for good reason: the church recognized that it had much to lose, so it summoned up all means necessary to maintain the status quo. The threat of loss, isolation, lack of security, humiliation, and pain wield tremendous power, ironically to both the oppressors and the oppressed! But to the oppressors, it manifests in anxious grabs for status-quo privilege, and to the oppressed, in fearful subjugation. Given that, a conversion is necessary, not just within the heart of the oppressor, but within the spirit of the victim: from fearfulness to empowerment. Baptist theologian Dwight Hopkins (1953–) teases out this truth: for someone to be free, fear must be relativized or overcome. This is not easy, not even a little bit. He writes:

> Fear stands at the root of the oppressed person's entrapment to macropolitical structures of discrimination and microspiritual demons of self-imposed restraints.

Working people fear the implications of struggling to claim the resources and wealth that God has given all humanity. Women face the physical strength of men; blacks (and other people of color) confront an entire edifice of white supremacy; and lesbians and gays experience the fickle and volatile whims of the entire heterosexual population. At the same time, the least in society experience a silent killer: the profound self-imposed fear acting as glue for self-doubt, low self-esteem, harmful anger, resentment, and lack of enough self-love.[14]

To add insult to injury, then, those who suffer oppression suffer a quadruple cut: not only are they treated with injustice, not only do they need to overcome fear to fend off the oppression, not only do they also have to slog through the internalized messages of diminishment that have been passed down through generations in order to reach the freedom that should have been theirs all along, but they also have to find the energy, the breath, if you will, to push beyond it all. Systems do not like change. The preservation of the status quo is the reigning system's goal, and suppression is its method.

Lynchings, like crucifixions, were one of the most effective means to maintain an evil system. Cone found New Testament scholar Paula Fredriksen's observation on point: "Crucifixion was a Roman form of public service announcement: Do not engage in sedition as this person has, or your fate will be similar. The point of the exercise was not the death of the offender as such, but getting the attention of those watching. Crucifixion first and foremost is addressed to an audience."[15] Intimidation keeps the systems running, keeps the oppressed in fear, keeps people believing that resistance is futile, and keeps people doubting their worth for anything other than the value established by the oppressor.

Justification and Sanctification

It is here that the gift of Luther's Reformation (re)discovery of justification anchors our new Reformation (re)discovery of justice. The craving to hear that we are liberated from fear and liberated from sin has not dissipated in this half a millennium. But increasingly, we realize that the scope of justification is and always has been broader than just forgiveness and freedom from condemnation. That said, this very justification, grounded in freedom, reminds us of our own worth and the worth of all creatures of God. Justification therefore leads to justice.

In this vein, African American theologian Albert Pero (1935–2015) taught that justification is fundamentally about self-affirmation. God's act of forgiveness for all people and the promise of new life for all people mean that we are invited to be dependent on that news above all other claims on our identity and worth. "Justification," he says, "means that African-Americans can be as fully human as God intends them to be."[16]

> Justification, grounded in freedom, reminds us of our own worth and the worth of all creatures of God.

Knowing that one is justified—defined by God's vision of us and not by alternate visions—frees a person to "be trimmed to the white light" of God's agenda for us and for the world, and only to God's agenda. In this sense, says Pero, African American theology teaches that justification is inherently holistic. It "is a process within God's purposeful activity to build a kingdom of justice, equity, and wholeness."[17] Whereas much of Western Christianity has concerned itself with an individual's relationship with God, African American theology sees the individual not as isolated from the whole but as both a representative and an integrated part of all people. Justified, we can't help but extend justice.

It is exactly at this point that Lutheranism has long balked. Why? Because, some have argued, even a whiff of the necessity of works—of doing something—threatens, ignores, or misses the point of being justified: we don't have to do anything to earn God's good grace.

But theologies from the underside—those that have been woefully underrepresented in predominantly white, mainstream theological conversation—see good works not as a *requisite* of God's love, but as a *sign and consequence* of God's love. Sufferers are committed to the scriptural witness of God being continually on the side of the forlorn, the forgotten, and the weak. And because sufferers see themselves in Jesus on the cross, and see Jesus on the cross in themselves, they know that God is in all suffering and with all sufferers. In fact, James Cone saw solidarity with those who suffer as an occasion of holy liberation. What, asks Cone, are the people of God about if not the cry "Set my people free"? He explains:

> When the meaning of sanctification is formed in the social context of an oppressed community in struggle for liberation, it is difficult to separate the experience of holiness from the spiritual empowerment to change the existing societal arrangements. If "I'm a child of God wid soul set free" because "Christ hab brought my liberty," then I will find it impossible to tolerate slavery and oppression. . . . The historical realization of the experience of salvation has always been an integral part of the black religious tradition.[18]

Liberation, sanctification, justification—black theology closely understands all of these expressions of the gospel as manifestations of salvation. In fact, they are entirely in keeping with the biblical understanding of *soteria*, of health, healing, and wholeness. In this theological framework, justification deals with the whole person and the whole people. It is about forgiveness, of course, but more than that, it is about setting people right before God; setting people free from sin, shame, and guilt; and releasing them from concession to and victimization by oppressive systems.

In fact, reducing justification and salvation to the forgiveness of sins, says Cynthia Crysdale, "will overpower those who have a broken sense of agency in the first place."[19] For example, abused women can be subjugated not only by the men in their lives, but also by the message that the abuse needs forgiveness rather than freedom from it. In this context, like so many of chronic suffering, the abuse persists, as does the despair that it can ever stop.

Hope

It is precisely for this reason, then, that for the black community, the Christian symbol of death, the cross, became a symbol of liberation and a symbol of hope. For Luther and many who have embraced his emphasis on grace, the primary source of hope the cross represents is the forgiveness of sins; for blacks, it became a symbol of Jesus's solidarity in the midst of suffering and of the promise of life when, for all the world, there was little but death to see and trust. As Cone says, when black Christians gathered at church, they were reminded that "trouble and sorrow would not determine our final meaning."[20]

It's quite easy, when we are suffering, to imagine that one's present moment and meaning are one's final enduring moment and meaning. Whether we are facing ecological disaster, national policies that create catastrophic consequences for the most vulnerable, a political climate that is toxic in the extreme, or grief due to deep, penetrating personal loss, we can feel profoundly hopeless. Despair is a victory for oppression and for death. But when hope stirs, when a faith-truth stands in the face of lived truth, defiant courage begins pushing back against despair. We recall that our suffering is not God's intention. Renewed in hope, we begin to be moved in spite of and to spite it all, to live into the fullest expression of who we individually and collectively are called to be.

Courage

Hope represents trust in something not lived, or at least not lived in its fullest expression. Insofar as that is true, hope is fundamentally subversive, for it threatens established power. Hope upheaves systems. Certainly, those who engaged in the resistance movement against the Nazis understood the risk involved in living out of hope rather than living into the palpable fear of the Third Reich. Speaking truth that engendered hope took subversive courage. As retired pastor and professor of German studies Dean Stroud says:

> To speak of Christ as the authentic Führer and, by implication, not Hitler, was subversive speech. To speak of sinners and not of victors was also subversive, for Nazis insisted on the victorious outcome of the cultural struggle during its first years and then later the victorious outcome of the war. To say something good about the people of the Old Testament or to identify Christ with the Jews or as a Jew was inflammatory rhetoric. To suggest that the weak and helpless were deserving of God's love and Christian charity was to go against the Nazi teaching about the mentally ill and the handicapped, whose lives did not have the same value as did the healthy and strong. To mention the suffering brought on by the war was to be a traitor who doubted the genius of the führer. To place God's kingdom above all earthly kingdoms (i.e., the Reich) was to side with the international conspiracy against the German *Volk*. And to alert the congregation

to the suffering of the Jews or to the suffering caused by the war was to place oneself in immediate danger.[21]

Many a rostered leader has experienced the accusation of "preaching politics" when, in fact, she or he is just preaching the text and preaching the gospel. These days, it takes courage to speak of Amos, Micah, Luke, and Matthew 25, to name a few biblical texts that turn heads! But for those who are there to hear a leader do so, for those who are desperate for hope and reason to persevere, this sort of preaching is not just balm for the soul. It is the good news, because it announces an ultimate reality that stands in stark contrast to the penultimate threat and reality of fear and death. Simply reminding people of an alternate truth injects hope into a world of despair. And it is not just good news to those living in fear or despair: those who cause suffering need to be freed from their oppressive ways. Truth realigns people's trust and their allegiance. It calls forth courage. In this way, hope is perhaps most essentially a matter of first-commandment enacted faith.

> Truth realigns people's trust and their allegiance. It calls forth courage.

Resistance

Max Lackmann (1910–2000) understood that courageous hope manifests itself as resistance. Lackmann was a German theologian and early member of the Confessing Church, the Christian body organized in protest of the Lutheran churches that had abdicated their identity to Hitler. In 1934, in the early years of Hitler's rule, he wrote an essay entitled "Lord, Where Shall We Go?" He authored it as a student to his student colleagues, warning that a fateful decision was before them: either they swore loyalty to the Nazis or loyalty to the gospel. The two, Lackmann said, were utterly incompatible claims on their allegiance.

In this epistle, Lackmann made clear that for these future leaders of the church, the stakes were high. As described by Stroud, they had to decide whether they would follow "'the Jew Jesus of Nazareth' or stand with the German *Volk* that wanted to follow its own 'longings and ideas.' The decision facing Christians in Germany in 1934 was simply the decision to proclaim the gospel—nothing more."[22] Lackmann's bold reminder (all the bolder because he was only a theology student) that Jesus was a Jew, coupled with his stark definition of the choice as being between membership in the German *Volk* and the community of Christ, sent him to Dachau concentration camp.

Lackmann isn't as well-known as another German Lutheran theologian, Dietrich Bonhoeffer, mentioned earlier in this book. Bonhoeffer also detected the dangers of the Nazi state and the fundamental contradiction between its laws and tenets and those of Jesus. Unfortunately, while respected as a young scholar, he was also seen as reactionary and cynical about Hitler and his power. His colleagues' dismissal of Bonhoeffer's warnings was born out of both their inability to comprehend the terrors that were to come and their own need for security, which Bonhoeffer's disruption threatened.

Bonhoeffer called it when he wrote about the nature of prophets:

> A prophet is a man who in a particular, earthshaking moment in his life knows himself seized and called by God, and now he can do no other than go among people and proclaim the will of God. His calling has become the turning point of his life, and there is only one thing left for him to do: to follow this calling, even if it may lead him into misfortune or into death. . . . The genuine prophet is not the one who always cries peace, peace, and victory, but the one who has the courage to proclaim disaster, says Jeremiah (Jer. 23:9ff.). . . . The central point from which one gains an understanding of the prophetic soul is the fact that the prophet knows himself in covenant with God, and this covenant makes his life a tragedy for him; because it is a covenant with God, the tragedy has an incomparable seriousness.[23]

Well-educated pastors and theologians who understood themselves to be faithful Christians, loyal to family, church, and nation, became either silent bystanders or active participants in Nazi atrocities, and for good reason. Who wants to "proclaim disaster," let alone make life a tragedy? Yet it is precisely what their professed faith in Christ required. Ours does too.

Martin Niemöller's famous words after World War II, displayed on the wall at the exit of the Holocaust Museum in Washington, DC, reflect by way of a confession the facile habit of silence as an acquiescent force:

First they came for the socialists, and I did not speak
out—because I was not a socialist.

Then they came for the trade unionists, and I did not
speak out—because I was not a trade unionist.

Then they came for the Jews, and I did not speak out—
because I was not a Jew.

Then they came for me—and there was no one left to
speak for me.[24]

Cynthia Moe-Lobeda knows that the socialist, the trade
unionist, and the Jews of our day, and in varying ways and
degrees, are threatened by acquiescent, accepted, and acceptable silence. And still now so are others:

What is the cultural violence that enables U.S. society
to normalize and accept the practice of paying CEOs
450 times the earnings of their lowest-paid workers,
especially when that wage does not meet the bare-bone
needs of food and shelter? What mesmerizing forces
of cultural violence make it desirable for Seattleites to
build huge luxurious houses while ignoring the city's six
to ten thousand homeless people and lobbying against
the movement to effect an income tax on the wealthiest
citizens of Washington State?[25]

Culturally and systemically, rather than losing our privilege, even
Christians will opt for this sort of "violence" in a heartbeat. Privileged lives depend on poverty. We may not like the existence of
poverty, but we dislike the loss of privilege even more.

Resistance calls for courage, but it must be courage that is stewarded by way of solidarity extended from those with the most to lose to those with the most to gain by way of equity, relief, and reason to hope.

Solidarity

A brief dive into etymology: the word *solidarity* comes from the French word *solidarité*, which means shared interests, responsibilities, and interdependance. *Solidarity* also comes from the yet older French *solide*, which means firm, dense, and compact, which in turn comes from the Latin *solidus*, which means firm, whole, and entire, itself related to the Latin word *salvus*, the Latin word from which we get *salvation*, meaning wholeness.

Roman Catholic theologian Jean Vanier (1928–2019) dedicated his life to L'Arche, a movement that creates communities bent toward creating solidarity between people with and without culturally defined disabilities. Vanier's years of being with people not just at the margins of society, but sometimes far beyond them, led him to see that when we are in solidarity with others, we are, in point of fact, in solidarity with God. As such, we simultaneously experience and offer salvation. He explains, "To become a friend of Jesus is to become a friend of the excluded. As we learn to be a friend of the excluded, we enter into this amazing relationship that is friendship with God."[26]

Bonhoeffer experienced this notion of solidarity, too, thanks to the invitation of the French pacifist and theologian Jean Lasserre and African American friend and pastor (and later dean of the School of Theology of Selma University) Albert Fisher to join the civil rights movement and join black churches. Because those men invited Bonhoeffer "into empathetic experiences . . . which enabled him to see broader implications of Jesus as *Stellvertretung* [representative for humanity]," his theology was jarred "loose from its captivity to nationalism."[27] Solidarity began to mean not just shared pain, but shared humility and shared experience of God. It is not too much, then, to imagine that Bonhoeffer's death on the gallows was not just his; his martyrdom was due to his solidarity with the Jews, gypsies, homosexuals, and persons of disability. Reggie Williams puts it this way:

> Solidarity began to mean not just shared pain, but shared humility and shared experience of God.

> In Harlem . . . the black Christ [was] despised and lynched time and again by white racist Christians, and in Germany Jesus was sent to Nazi gallows and gas chambers. Christians in Germany failed to hear Bonhoeffer's early warnings; they did not understand the dangers he was pointing out to them. They simply were not equipped with the same perceptive insight. But Bonhoeffer would not have seen the danger so clearly either, and he may have avoided his fate at Flossenbürg that Monday morning in April, in solidarity with Christ, if it were not for his experience in the Harlem Renaissance

that validated the cosufferer image in human practice as he learned to act on behalf of the hungry, the poor, and the downtrodden, marginalized members of every human context.[28]

Bonhoeffer realized that theological theorizing wasn't immediately redemptive; it did not bring tangible *soteria*—health, healing, or wholeness—to him or anyone else. Solidarity in motion, however, was redemptive.

In 1933, Bonhoeffer presented "The Church and the Jewish Question" to a roomful of Berlin pastors. In it, he detailed three ways that the church can engage the state. First, it can ask the state whether it is being responsible to its commitment to its citizens. Second, it can stand beside those who are victimized by the state. And last and perhaps most famously, he said the church's role "is not just to bandage the victims under the wheel, but to jam a spoke in the wheel itself."[29] Those words speak directly to this very moment, now eighty-some years later. Bonhoeffer was convinced that the church is to be a purveyor of prophetic word and prophetic action. His conviction is entirely in keeping with a staple teaching of liberation theology, one that Lutheran theologian Craig Nessan (1952–) describes as a hope to create a people of God eager to "lead theology out of the academic environment and the church out of the sanctuary."[30] This is no message of anti-intellectualism; it is a message of anti-elitism.

For some, taking this step isn't a choice; it is a pull. Faith that does not translate piety into liberating action simply has no heft, no relevance. Bonhoeffer issued this same hard-won wisdom from prison, and it still reverberates to the Christians of a post-Hitler world: "For your thought and action will enter on a new relationship; your thinking will be confined to your responsibilities in action. With us, thought was often the luxury of the onlooker; with you it will be entirely subordinated to action."[31]

Church

For all that Lutherans turn to Paul as the quintessential proclaimer of grace over works, New Testament theologian Lyle Vander Broek points out that Paul does not seem to be particularly interested in faith that is private. Rather, the Spirit in Paul regularly calls forth community—community in relationship with, even dependent on, one another. The gifts so famously listed as of the Spirit are inherently corporal in purpose, given "for the common good" (1 Cor 12:7). Pauline thought sees that, as followers of Jesus, we are, as individuals and as a community, images of God (Rom 8:17–30; 2 Cor 3:18; Eph 4:24; Col 3:10). Insofar as that is true, the church's dedication to the well-being of the other is a reflection of God's love for us as individuals and as a collective. We embody in word and deed the life, death, and resurrection of Jesus, the quintessential expression of God's agenda for the world. We are gospel in motion, conforming not to this age (Rom 12:2) but to the proleptic promises of God, injecting God's future into the present, spreading hope, liberation, justification, and justice where people and places yearn for each.[32]

This dedication to communal well-being as church isn't just solid theology; it also is solid social theory. Social theorist Erich Fromm investigated the phenomenon of conformity with the powers of this world when fascism and totalitarianism were on the rise. According to Moe-Lobeda, "His findings attribute that acquiescence in part to an 'individualized view' of life, an inability to perceive the broader societal dimensions of personal life. He called for 'a structuralized picture of the world' as a necessary ingredient in action for social change toward 'a social order governed by the principles of equality, justice and love.'"[33] Albeit using secular terms, Fromm described a key facet of life in the church: we are not meant to be alone, we are not meant to suffer (alone or not), and we are not meant to leave people alone.

It is much like what we see in Acts 2:44—a community bent on ensuring that all have enough, precisely because it believes that Jesus is risen. It's much like what the church is within oppressed communities and what it could be on a grand, broad scale. Liberation theology, for example, has lived out this new Reformation coming long before the white, Western church lifting up the well-being of the entire community as a, if not *the*, basic theological impulse and expression of its movement. Social-justice action is keenly explicit here as the *primary* calling of the church, explicitly manifest in the direct engagement with political forces in the world: "Theology must, in lieu of Latin American poverty, surrender its futile attempts to remain politically neutral and make a conscious decision for a politics which takes the side of justice for the poor."[34]

Conclusion

Anand Giridharadas is an author and a political and cultural analyst. His parents immigrated to the United States from India, he grew up in Ohio, and he has dedicated much of his recent professional life to analyzing the current political, social, and cultural dynamics in the United States. The entrenched divide we are experiencing in the States, he says, could be appreciated with more compassion were we to appreciate the underlying fears driving the competing perspectives. In an interview, he said:

> "Understand the fear behind something" is often taken to excuse or forgive it. But I'm not saying that. From time to time I'm told, "Go back to your country!" or "Where are you from?" And I fight it with every ounce of ferocity to which I'm entitled. But understand where it's coming from. Understand that there are people who were born into a country in which their social world was 96 percent white and men ran everything. Frankly, they never got the memo about a new world that was coming. They feel lost. Bereft. And the condition of having that kind of fear and pain is often being unable to say that you have fear and pain.[35]

His words remind me yet again of the scriptural refrain: "Do not be afraid." But that does not mean there is nothing about which to be afraid. Those who are fearing the loss of power will, demographically, lose power. That is already clear and drives all the more the protectionism and anger. But it takes little imagination—yet lots of compassion—to recognize that not just power, but also a way of life, will be lost. As Giridharadas says elsewhere:

> Americans today are bobbing in a roiling ocean of change. Donald Trump is merely a barnacle on a shell in an estuary off that ocean. A big, messy, powerful country, with high ideals and a history of trying and failing and trying again to realize them, is being remade. The idea of an American is being rewritten. People seldom listened to are taking center stage.
>
> It's a lot. We all need a little grace. Those who await the country that is coming might recall how hard it is to surrender what you have long possessed, even if it wasn't rightly yours. Seeing those marooned from an older America, the woke might throw them a raft and pull those willing to be saved into the next country. And those who fear and resent this new America in the making might consider how it has felt all these years not to be part of the dream, wholly or at all, and might conclude that they have a stake in making the country what they have always imagined it to be. It will take grace— and work.[36]

All of his insights are so very helpful, here, but I find it fascinating and ever so helpful that Giridharadas uses the language of faith here: grace and works. His observations and his language are wise not just for our country, but also for this moment in Christian history.

We, too, are at a theological juncture. We are in dire need of the grace that Luther's announcement of justification offered us. We also need the works of justice that extend from this justification. Economic justice, climate justice, human rights justice, gender justice, racial justice—all have to do with the fundamental worthiness of everyone and everything created in the image of God, and all have to do with the consequent justice that everyone and everything therefore deserves.

There is, in God's eyes, no separation of church and state. Each relates to the other, informs the other, and shapes the other. As Hopkins says, this is a moment—I'd say a new Reformation moment—when "the Spirit of liberation with us, Jesus, heralds the dawning of intense and persistent efforts towards social transformation . . . . The spiritual is political and the political is spiritual."[37]

> We also need the works of justice that extend from this justification.

Discussion Questions

1. Name some ways our world today differs from the world Luther knew. These might include differences that are cultural, social, economic, political, and/or ecclesiastical (pertaining to the church).

2. What critique of the hymn "In the Sweet By and By" does the author lift up? How does looking at Jesus's life through the lens of the Gospels address this critique?

3. The author also lifts up black theology and its perspective on Jesus's suffering. What can be learned from this perspective, especially as it relates to salvation or *soteria*?

4. What, if any, new perspectives did you learn in the author's discussion of sin? Choose a particular statement with which you strongly agree or disagree. Explain why the statement strikes you this way.

5. How does the author expand her understanding of justification beyond the forgiveness of sins? How does she suggest justification and justice are related?

6. According to the author, how do hope and courage play a role in taking a stand against injustice? Have you ever experienced injustice of any kind? If you wish, tell your story. Where did you find hope or courage?

7. What struck you about the author's perspectives on resistance and solidarity?

8. "Social justice action is keenly explicit here as the primary calling of the church" (page 112). The author calls this perspective a new Reformation moment. In what ways do you agree with this? In what ways do you challenge this view?

5

Here We Stand

I write this chapter on Reformation Day 2018. Typically, on this day, Lutherans will reach into the back of our closets to get dressed in the most brilliant red outfit we own, and we look forward to the sanctuary color spectrum: splashes of crimsons and currants and scarlets and sangrias and burgundies and merlots and the occasional E-for-Effort magenta pinks or rusty oranges. We are humming "A Mighty Fortress" even before we get to the car. But yesterday, the very day before Reformation Day, the Squirrel Hill Synagogue shooter let loose. He sprayed the holy space with bullets and death because, as he said later at the hospital (while being treated by Jewish doctors), this man wanted all Jews to die, and Jews were committing genocide by supporting refugees. In earlier social-media accounts, he called Jews by derogatory names, insulting them as "filthy" and "evil," referring to them as an "infestation." At so many levels, of course, there is cause for deep dismay at the murderous rampage, one that occurred in the same week as various liberal politicians, along with media and entertainment personalities, received bombs delivered to their homes and offices.

We are grieving today. No fortress is so mighty this side of kingdom come that evil can't slip in. It is a particularly poignant event for Lutherans aware of the troubled history of Luther and the Jews. Making the juxtaposition of this anti-Semitic violence with the celebration of Reformation Day caused additional heartache.

It's a fact less known than it should be that Luther was not only a reformer, but also anti-Semitic. Despite scholars' attempts to relativize and contextualize his consistently jaded views on Jews or to partition off his words as only or most flamboyantly located in his latter writings, Luther was shamefully and unabashedly anti-Jewish. In a short but powerful column in *Currents*, Craig Nessan establishes a solid and disturbing list of instances in which Martin Luther engaged in racial slander, theological malfeasance against the Jewish tradition, and outright racial and religious bigotry against Jews. Be it by distorting Jewish history and theology (e.g., LW 25:380, 385–86, 413) or by making crass ad hominem attacks (LW 25:395–96, 405, 425), Luther's diatribe and rhetoric against Jews contributed to a large, historic vat filled with a slurry of anti-Semitic hate and violence.[1]

Luther was a mix of a man, filled with great insight and great blindness. Luther's incongruent anti-Semitism necessitates reflection on factors that contributed to his skewed opinions about Jews and the Jewish faith, and to that end Dr. Alon Goshen-Gottstein, scholar of interfaith and religious studies, even has crafted a list he calls "The Luther Model." It pulls together and ponders the constellation of components that led to Luther's hate-filled views. Luther, says Goshen-Gottstein, was influenced by the following seven factors, which are transferable to other instance of bigotry and prejudice.

1. Lack of contact with Jews and no meaningful first-hand knowledge of Jews.
2. Wrong and misleading knowledge and information concerning Jews and Judaism.
3. Personal hurt and offense, as a consequence of deep religious engagement. Luther had been deeply hurt by how Jews had referred to his God.
4. Personal trauma and personal fears.
5. Theological and scriptural foundations. Luther was guided by his reading of Scripture to the conviction that only in Jesus could salvation be found.
6. Protecting Christian identity and authenticity. Luther took badly the reports of Jews converting Christians.
7. The apocalyptic dimension. Luther felt he was living at the end of time and was fighting the final battle. This led to his taking more extreme positions.[2]

While this series of observations contains incredibly helpful insights into Luther's bigoted notions about Jews, the list also details how prejudice and then consequential prejudicial action take place: a lack of relationship with the loathed, misinformation, personal affront, phobias, religious belief, protectionism, and fear. I believe we have gotten to this point in our political and civil discourse today based on precisely these factors and some variations on the themes.

What, though, is this present point? Broadly, it is a combination of complex, intense, pressing trends and events that are shaping lives and deaths and history. Their specifics matter, though, because they are both symptoms and problems, both factors and manifest consequence, of the new Reformation moment in which we find ourselves. As we reflect on what the gospel is and means in this new time, it is as necessary to be as mindful of our context as when we dove deeply into Luther's.

Our Present Moment

In 2008, Phyllis Tickle's book *The Great Emergence: How Christianity Is Changing and Why* was published. With her customary knack for weaving beautiful prose and astute perceptiveness, Tickle (1934–2015) swept her scholarship over the last two thousand years and noticed something: about every five hundred years, a significant transition occurs. These transitions take place not only between eras, but between fundamental ways of seeing and being in the world.

The era inaugurated by Jesus's life Tickle dubbed the Great Transformation. This was followed by the period of Gregory the Great, the Dark Ages, and the rise of monasticism. Next came the period dominated by the Great Schism that divided Western Roman Catholic and Eastern Orthodox branches of Christianity. Luther's advent marks the next period, the Great Reformation.

Five hundred years following Luther's time, we now live in the next era, which is just beginning—not that we are yet clear about what this era is exactly. Even for this ambiguous state, Dr. Tickle has some words of wisdom: "It is the religious shifts that ultimately will inform and interpret all the others. . . . [It] is sufficient to say that this thing is a-borning, and it is we who must faithfully and prayerfully attend to its birthing."[3] Because of that, Tickle named it the Great Emergence.

No facet of an era's experience can be strictly isolated from another, of course. Each epoch shift reveals a confluence of fundamental reevaluations and re-formations within the components of culture, economics, knowledge, politics, philosophies, and religion. But though specific issues of each period obviously differ, the fundamental questions behind them all remain the same: Where, now, is the authority? Who are we now, and by what or whom will we be defined?

Again, I am convinced that for Christians, it's essentially a first-commandment question: To whom do we bow? The authority that Luther called into question was the church. But in a surprise twist, Luther's advent redefined the authority so that ultimately it became the self, its private interpretation of the Bible, and its own privatized faith. But now, in our age, this individualism is being profoundly questioned. Suddenly, the bifurcation of the self and the other, the secular and the religious, no longer makes sense or is workable.

> Who are we now, and by what or whom will we be defined?

This chapter is dedicated to some of the tremendous forces and dynamics in play and at hand in our present Great Emergence, including glances at the tragedies that occur when we see ourselves as separate from others. The things "a-dying" are causing the most angst, and violent angst at that. Many fear the loss of privilege and decry institutional change. Even the established understandings of church are undergoing a kind of death. Much is being lost, with much more to lose, bringing not just insecurity but also the desperate grasping of what was, as if it will and should always be.

And so I will offer a brief glance, then, at some of the factors and forces of our present emergence. It helps to recall Luther's theology-of-the-cross conviction that only by calling a thing what it is can we be free, for the diagnosis is dire. The following description is without a doubt discouraging, even depressing. But with the conviction of the resurrection, the prognosis carries, in fact, some hope for new possibilities, new ways, and new life.

Climate Change and Environmentalism

There is no way around it: the present state of the earth's health is distressing. Paul Crutzen (1933–), a Nobel Prize–winning atmospheric chemist, maintains that humans have now managed to single-handedly usher in a new geological age. While Tickle divided world history according to eras determined by events, Crutzen and other scientists determine ages according to climate and extinction rates. For about twelve thousand years, the earth has enjoyed what the scientific community calls the Holocene Age; it means, etymologically, the New Whole Age, marked by the retreat of the glaciers in the Paleolithic Age and the consequent advent of humans.

But it is precisely humans who have ended the very age they inaugurated. Human activity, population growth, and energy consumption have all created this new age, dubbed by Crutzen the Anthropocene, the Age of the Human.[4] No one is quite sure or quite agrees when it took hold (when the Industrial Age began? the Atomic Age?), but few dispute *that* it has taken hold. Atmospheric carbon levels due to the burning of fossil fuels are on the rise. The rate of deforestation, due to building new homes and businesses and increased farming, speeds up the rate of global warming. Without the trees, excess carbon cannot be absorbed. That means carbon, as well as methane, is becoming trapped in the atmosphere, causing greenhouse gases, or sinking into the oceans, causing increased acidic levels in the seas, threatening most especially corals and shelled creatures. All of this yields dramatic increases in temperatures. In the last hundred years, the average global temperature has increased 1.4 degrees, and sixteen out of the seventeen hottest years on record have been since 2000.

Behind these statistics hide fundamental changes in global ecosystems. Extreme weather events like hurricanes, blizzards, droughts, floods, and fires are becoming the norm. Polar melts are threatening not only the polar bears but humans, too. We don't know what microbes are being or will be released, and the melting glaciers also cause sea levels to rise; they've risen as much as eight inches since 1870, threatening communities and cultures on the coasts.

As if that weren't enough, the rising temperatures, waters, and rates of extreme weather incidents are changing migration patterns and ecosystems. Species are having to move to find weather more suitable to their needs; unfortunately, this process alone threatens their existence and exposes them to new environmental or creaturely threats. Humans also are affected by weather patterns; farmers are being forced to adapt crops or move them, a process that may or may not affect the yields. When food sources are threatened or disappear, peace and stability also are called into question.

Plastics, a word and a way of life made famous in the 1967 movie *The Graduate*, cause tremendous trouble for humans and for wildlife. Single-use bags, bottles, straws, and utensils cannot decompose and will last in whole or in broken-down pieces for hundreds, if not thousands, of years. To boot, the cancer-causing chemicals (such as nitrogen and phosphorus) within them leech into the soils and waterways, and it is only a matter of time before humans and wildlife ingest them.

In recent years, one response has been to pull back many of the protections offered to fish, wildlife, water, land, air, and people, erring on the side of protecting our way of life. Regulations have been rescinded, sacred lands of Native communities have been forsaken, and the science that has driven decisions and policies has been not just ignored but prevented from seeing the light of day. There is increasing deep concern that we lack an appreciation of the desperate nature of our situation and that we have passed a point of no return, from which neither science nor even God can turn us back.

The trouble is, the sub-issues of climate change are hardly black and white. For example, fossil fuels power our cars, our hospitals, our homes, and the very iPad that is on my lap. The people who work in the fields or the mines or the trains or the ships of the oil and mining industries have a life and a culture built by and around these industries. These people need a trade and a livelihood as much as anyone. It is powerfully difficult, then, to reconcile the effects of air pollution, water pollution, and land pollution with the economies and ways of life that have become part of the essence of who we are and how we live.

What does the church have to say to this dire, complicated, pressing reality of human-caused climate change? Interestingly, although the Old Testament is lush with imagery about cherishing and stewarding the land, that message of creation care is far less pronounced in the New Testament. Some speculation about this silence centers on the fact that the early Christians were certain that Jesus was coming back at any moment. As such, they focused more on spreading God's word, prior to this imminent return, and less on the cultivation of God's world.

Delving into the early texts of the Old Testament may give us more direct references and direction about our immediate role and responsibilities for the well-being of earth and its inhabitants. Perhaps no verse has been more consequential than Genesis 1:28, which contains God's command that humankind "be fruitful and multiply, and fill the earth and subdue it; and have dominion over the fish of the sea and over the birds of the air and over every living thing that moves upon the earth." Its influence reveals much of how humanity sees itself and its relationship to creation, particularly due to a rueful misunderstanding of one word, which in turn has led to rueful misunderstandings of both humanity and creation.

The word *radah*, which is translated as "dominion," does indeed mean to have power over. This word is used any number of times in the Old Testament with both benevolent and malevolent meanings. But in *this* place, where the context is one of creation, of abundance, and of God's creatures being "good," the word implies a message of tending, rather than rending.

However, the earth has been rent. We have now reached a moment where optimism may no longer be of help; we are in the realm of hope. This is also the realm of the church, for we are nothing if not people of hope. We are now in a moment of hope and of repentance and reform, called to recognize that all of God's creation is justified and worthy in God's sight, and therefore worthy of justice. An active and persistent congregational biblical and theological study about eco-justice could help ground our care of the earth not into political identities but into religious identities.

> We are now in a moment of hope and of repentance and reform.

Earth justice, as an act of faith, looks both simple and complex: eating lower on the food chain; buying fuel-efficient cars, riding bikes, or taking public transportation; lowering the carbon footprint of your home and your congregation by analyzing your energy output; spending time in the outdoors to learn to love it. These are all small ways that individuals and congregations can "have dominion" over the earth and thereby save it. However, there are other ways to tend to the earth by way of activism: lobbying for alternative and renewable energy sources, advocating for carbon taxes, publicly supporting politicians who acknowledge that climate change is real, and engaging in strikes or marches. Each can be a faithful response, actively tending to the earth as an act of faith and an act of justice.

Fake News and Distrust of Science

In October 2017, Donald Trump claimed that he had invented the term *fake news*. He didn't, of course; it was a term that can be traced to the late 1800s. As an intentional tactic, the term has manipulated people's opinions and political allegiances for centuries. What Trump did do, of course, was to popularize the term and attempt to cast doubt on all news.

So-called fake news can take the form of satire, as *The Onion* and late-night comics create so masterfully. But as a tool, real fake news (an awkward term at best) is a tremendously effective method of spreading propaganda dressed as actual news. To call it effective, however, is to understate its power: fake news has the capacity to undermine civility and established scientific truth, skew elections, and even threaten democracy.

Although mass communication and fake news have been bedfellows for some time, the advent of the internet ratcheted up the scale and potency of the phenomenon. Anyone can set up a legitimate blog or a website; anyone can set up a duplicitous one, too. Blogs and websites are largely unregulated, and the fusion of these truths can make it difficult to determine which are legitimate sources and which are suspect (Snopes has been often a helpful corrective to this new reality!). An additional disconcerting factor is that algorithms for news or social media feeds hone advertisements to the established interests and opinions of the individual user, creating what have come to be known as "filter bubbles": increasingly curated images of reality that reinforce rather than expand one's point of view. Recently, Russia has been in the news for essentially weaponizing these possibilities by creating highly polished and inflammatory sites, posts, and clickbait that target people susceptible to the information on them.

Distressingly, studies demonstrate that fake news has more traction than real news. According to *The Atlantic*, fake news goes viral six times faster than a real story, and it is retweeted more within online niches: nineteen retweets to every ten of authentic news. That's an incredible viral power. Why? Fake news is sexier, seems more epic, and is crafted to inspire a visceral response that lends itself to action.[5] Used as a political tool, fake news fans vitriol, hate, and extremism—and does so not least of all by calling the integrity of the Fourth Estate, the news media, into deep question.

The term *post-truth* has been used to describe this phenomenon in which objective facts are less influential than appeals to emotion or personal belief in shaping public opinion. The post-truth phenomenon breeds suspicion, making distrust of what used to be trusted a contagious reaction. Even science, the hallmark litmus test (so to speak) of what is true and real and what is not, is coming into its own crisis of credibility. We see it perhaps most clearly in the dismissal and disputation of the science behind global warming and climate change. But in recent years, statistical data regarding taxes, immigration, employment, and income also have been removed from government websites or selectively suppressed.

As fact-based as science is supposed to be, facts too can be in the eye of the beholder. Although some conservatives have been most markedly suspicious about science, liberals too have called out science—or at least the researchers, whose own latent or manifest biases due to political agendas, personal presumptions, or funding sources can skew results. Together, however, the increasing distrust of science and the spreading of fake news create an additional element of uncertainty: What can be trusted?

It's an odd place for the Christian church to stand: we are people who speak of faith—something that, by definition, does not mean fact. In other words, I do not need faith to believe in something that is demonstrably true: it is a fact that the sun rises in the east, but it is an act of faith to book an appointment in one's calendar for tomorrow. Faith allows Christians to believe in a man who was dead and is now alive, but while there are facts surrounding this belief, no science will "prove" the resurrection.

We live, though, in a world of facts that we ignore to our peril—and to the peril of the world. Perhaps for people of faith, the matter of truth is ultimately a matter of the first commandment: Is what we are hearing aligned with what we understand God's agenda to be, or is it more aligned with what *our* agenda might be? On what basis are we giving credence to or dismissing news and scientific information: our hearings or God's callings? Is it possible to hold competing truths in civil tension (e.g., fossil fuels harm the environment and human health, and they provide jobs, save lives, and fuel our way of life)? And is it possible to lean into new truths (e.g., as difficult as a shift in the systems might be, alternative energy is less toxic to creation, could provide just as much energy for an indefinite amount of time, and would depend on similar skill sets of those now employed in carbon-based fuel industries)?

It seems that as we now question what truth is, an opportunity is before us to actively draw upon different ways of knowing. Facts are important, but so are intuition, empathy, and vision. Perhaps what we need more than anything is wisdom, so well expressed in the Hebrew word *yada*, rendered in English "to know," but with the sense of intimacy, the likes of which partners understand in their exchanges of love. Fused together, these forms of knowledge—facts, intuition, empathy, vision, wisdom—create a moment for the church to be poised to recognize and embrace both these notions: truth does not defy faith, and faith can inform our interpretation of truth. We will err, no doubt, but it becomes all the more necessary then to recall that we are nonetheless justified, worthy in God's sight, and worthy of justice grounded in that very truth.

> Truth does not defy faith, and faith can inform our interpretation of truth.

Poverty and Wealth

There is no more persistent and consistent theme in Scripture than care of the poor. Spanning Old and New Testaments, the cadence of concern about the impoverished and the vulnerable never lets up. Distressingly, it seems that poverty never lets up either.

Despite many presumptions about poor people, their circumstances are largely not their fault. In our country, a grand majority of people receiving public assistance work. Those who are not employed are often sick or disabled or tending to a family member who is. People living in poverty live in impoverished neighborhoods—a truism, but one that shapes not only the people's present but their future too. Those who live within these clusters of poverty have access to schools, homes, and safe havens of lower quality and greater risk than wealthier neighborhoods on the other side of the tracks. Even access to polling places is affected, not least of all because of gerrymandering, a reality that also shapes whether policies that benefit the poor are enacted or not. Poverty simply begets poverty; one's zip code foretells one's future.

Additionally, low minimum-wage rates exacerbate high poverty rates: earning the minimum wage for forty hours of work a week offers income well below the poverty line for two or more. That many minimum-wage positions do not offer health benefits, nor allowances for sick leave, family care leave, emergency leave, or, of course, a vacation only compounds the problem. Poverty generates poverty, just as wealth generates wealth. Money can be invested, which makes more money, which can be spent on a home, which in turn builds up equity and can be sold at a higher price than when it was bought, with profits being plowed into an upgraded home or into a loan to start a business. If you are poor, none of these are options.

The Urban Institute Survey of Consumer Finances revealed that whites in their thirties are on average $147,000 wealthier (with net assets three times greater) than blacks; by their sixties, they are $1.1 million wealthier, with seven times the assets of blacks. This gap can also be evaluated by way of lifetime income measures: on average, white men earn $2.7 million during their working years, black men earn $1.8 million, and Latinos earn $2.0 million. Gender distinctions are unfavorable to females: white women earn $1.5 million during their careers, black women $1.3 million, and Latinas $1.1 million. Intensifying the disadvantage for black Americans, the student loan debt carried by black families is significantly higher as well. With less access to family wealth to fund their education, these students more often turn to loans. These distinctions continue into retirement years. Compared with white workers, blacks and Hispanics have fewer access points to and less participation in employer retirement plans.[6]

Poverty and its effects strike across the globe: More than three million people—one-third of the world's population—live in poverty. Twenty-two thousand children die every day, according to UNICEF, not least of all due to a lack of access to clean water and malnutrition. Abroad as in the United States, a lack of financial security leads to a lack of housing security and a lack of educational security, which lead to a further lack of financial security. Wealth is just as stark a reality, but in a more concentrated fashion: 70.1 percent of the world's wealth is held by only 3 percent of the world's people; in the United States, 1 percent of the people own 40 percent of the wealth.[7]

We know that Scripture considers neither wealth nor poverty as a virtue, for neither represents God's vision for humanity. US culture, informed by the principle that monetary success reveals God's blessing, has historically seen wealth as a sign of God's grace and intended destiny. This view implies that poverty is a mark of God's disdain.

But the church and individual Christians are now called to speak vociferously against economic disparity, calling a thing what it is: a scourge and a deviation from God's vision of equity and security for all. The church and Christians are also being called to question the underlying systems that both create and enable poverty, and to engage more actively in subverting them. Capitalism itself is coming under the microscope, tax plans that benefit the rich are undergoing scrutiny, and democratic socialism—with increasing references to Christian influences— is gaining in popularity.

Now is the moment for the church and Christians to reflect on the relationship between our faith and economic justice and to reform inaction into action. Using the leadership and direction of denominational advocacy groups; following the lead of faith-based groups such as the Poor People's Campaign, Bread for the World, and Habitat for Humanity; voting for politicians who have as a basic element of their platforms economic equity; establishing or participating in food banks; and getting involved in organizations that offer low- and no-interest loans to low-income people are but some of the ways that Christians can announce that all are justified, worthy in God's sight, and therefore worthy of justice.

Women's Rights

Whether it be via #MeToo, #TimesUp, pink pussy hats, women leaning in, or the Women's March, women are engaged in a wave of feminist action that brings one's memory back to the 1970s. Fifty years have passed. The ERA hasn't yet. Women are now in a new moment in which new energy, new techniques, new platforms, and new boldness are all employed for new times to confront old and new issues.

White women still earn seventy-seven cents to the white man's dollar; for African American women, it's only sixty-four cents, and for Latinas, fifty-six cents. Add basic biology to this income inequity, and we get a host of hurdles to women's financial and vocational opportunity and security. Women who bear children must take time off from their educational or professional tracks for the birth of every child, and they often take more time to care for the son or daughter until school, because for many women, daycare is unaffordable. For certain professions that depend on higher education and routine advancements based on professional output, networking, and copious hours, pregnancy, birthing, and child rearing take a toll on the pace of promotion, which, in turn, takes a toll also on life-time earned income and retirement security—some estimate to the tune of half a million to a million dollars by the age of fifty-nine.[8]

Globally, girls and women face even more challenges. In many parts of the world, resistance to educating girls, child marriage, and lack of access to birth control and to proper medical care during birth cause severe financial, vocational, and personal crises. Girls and women face a chronic threat of sexual violence. Nearly one in five women are raped in their lifetime, nearly half suffer sexual assault, and nearly all experience some form of sexual harassment. Women suffer workplace discrimination, and many feel compelled to align their bodies with cultural expectations of beauty. Women have a far higher rate of single-parenting responsibilities: 82 percent of single parents are women. That these are still issues well into the twenty-first century demonstrates how intransigent these patterns are.

Humanity was created from *adamah*, or "soil"—a feminine noun in Hebrew! From it, "male *and* female [God] created them" (Gen 1:27). From this beginning, we see examples of gender equity dappled through scriptural history: Miriam, Deborah, Esther, the queens of Sheba and Chaldea, Mary the mother of Jesus, Mary Magdalene, Jesus teaching women, Jesus being taught by women, the first (and female) preachers at the tomb of Jesus, Phoebe, Junia, the pronouncement echoing from Joel into Paul that sons *and* daughters will prophesy, and the assurance that in Christ there is no male or female (Gal 3:28). Given that none of these texts were written at times when women's rights were a recognizable thing, it is astounding that that these references exist at all.

By way of lifting up women's history in Scripture, a feminist and womanist hermeneutic about Scripture, and women's leadership in the church, Christians can be all the more actively vocal about the equal role of women in the life of the church and in faith. Congregations can also offer safe places for women in abusive relationships, making clear that women are to be believed in instances of sexual assault. They can offer child-care resources to single mothers. Individuals can create circles of strong women to mentor each other and girls becoming women, support microloans to women on the edge of poverty, and affirm a girl's sense of self and vision of self.

> We are now in a moment when women's equality is more in reach than ever before.

We are now in a moment when women's equality is more in reach than ever before. The church is in a moment when our engagement and advocacy can be reformed to be more vocal that women are justified, declared worthy in God's sight, and therefore worthy of justice.

Sexuality and Gender

For a tragic reason, we can mark the 1980s as the decade in which people within the LGBTQIA (lesbian, gay, bisexual, transgender, queer—though sometimes understood as questioning—intersex, and asexual) community began to be seen, heard, acknowledged, and embraced by the heterosexual community and culture. AIDS initiated this cultural shift around sexuality and gender. This horrific disease not only touched those whom it infected, but also the family and friends who loved them. Consequently, fierce stereotypes and bigotry began to be transformed into fierce solidarity and respect, and now a coming out is often met with a shrug and a conversation about the weather.

Still, the struggle for those within the LGBTQIA community persists and, one could say, is in recent years all the more heightened. Repeated attempts to ban transgender military members, the move to reject legal acknowledgment (and thereby protection) of transgender people, the judicial approval to discriminate against LGBTQIA people based on religious principles (whether for cakes, a condo, or medical care), and the halting of the issuance of spousal visas to LGBTQIA diplomats in same-sex partnerships (rather than marriages, which is a universally available option for straight couples but, depending on country, is not for same-sex couples), there is a new wave of worry within this community. Although Matthew Shepard was finally laid to rest in the National Cathedral, no less, the recent rise of violence such as was suffered at the Orlando night club Pulse in 2016 leaves many in that community anxious and alert. But as is often the case with disparaged, maligned, and threatened groups, their attackers are driven by fear that morphs into disdain and hate. In the case of LGBTQIA bigotry, it is a fear of breaking what is believed to be an immutable religious and natural law, a fear of redefining what has been presumed to be a sexual norm, and because gay and transgender men seem to suffer the most discrimination, perhaps a fear of anything that is feminine.

In this day, how is the church a-borning being called to participate in sex and gender justice? Religiously, not only do LGBTQIA issues challenge a predominant and privileged reading of Scripture, but they also raise related hermeneutical issues: If *this* interpretation is wrong, what else in my faith might not be what I had believed to be infallibly true? The domino effect of rereading Scripture with a lens of sex and gender justice can be powerfully and contagiously disorienting, as reorientation often is. Establishing a congregation as an open and affirming community, rejecting conversion therapies (touted by some conservative religious organizations, though being banned in an increasing number of states and repudiated synods like my own, the Northeastern Minnesota Synod), lifting up "out" sisters and brothers to leadership roles, establishing gender-neutral bathrooms in churches—all are ways of advancing welcome and justice. Now is the moment to reform oppressive and bigoted views about LGBTQIA people, long held in the church, and to see that they are justified, worthy in God's sight, and therefore worthy of justice.

> Now is the moment to reform oppressive and bigoted views about LGBTQIA people.

Immigration, Racism, Religious Bigotry

Unless we belong to the First Nations, the indigenous peoples, we or our ancestors came by way of immigrationor captivity; arriving via ocean or land. Most recent immigrants come from Mexico, followed by people from Europe, Canada, the Caribbean, Central America, South America, and finally the Middle East and sub-Saharan Africa. Despite recent hostile rhetoric, immigrants commit less crime than native citizens, contribute $2 trillion to the US gross domestic product, and use public assistance at a lower rate than US-born citizens.[9] The majority come permitted to work, and of these, most (65 percent) are employed—a rate 6 percent higher than for the general US population.

However, particularly in the years following the 9/11 terrorist attacks, immigrants (especially nonwhite immigrants) are the recipients of tremendous racism and stereotypes. The rhetoric surrounding the purported necessity of a wall on the southern US border, for example, is based less on facts and more on mischaracterizations (indeed, lies) about the methods of those crossing, the violent tendencies of those crossing, the motivations of those crossing, the drain on the US economy were they to be allowed to cross, and statistics related to crime once those who have crossed are here. As a result, US policy has allowed the children of immigrants who had been given legal status to be deported, families to be separated at the border, and children to be taken away from parents at the border in the name of national security. Horrifyingly, this brutality has been done even in the name of God, as when former attorney general Jeff Sessions invoked Romans 13 as reason for us to trust the government's decision to remove babies from their caregivers.

The ugliness of racism is fully in play here. One doesn't need to be a recent immigrant, however, to experience racism. We see it when we increase our awareness of police tactics and a court system that profile and disproportionately punish African Americans. It is evident from the Ku Klux Klan and other right-wing groups holding larger and more public rallies and from the skyrocketing incidents of hate crimes targeting people of color and of non-Christian beliefs. It grows in the Petri dish of fear and anger expressed by political rhetoric that casts people from Mexico as criminals and rapists, people from Haiti as all being infected with AIDS, and the countries of Africa as being "shitholes."

Religious bigotry is also on the rise: the Pew Research Center tells us that in 2016, violence and acts of intimidation against Muslims surpassed the number of incidents immediately following 9/11,[10] and the Anti-Defamation League reports that between 2016 and 2017, the rate of anti-Semitic acts increased a whopping 57 percent—the largest leap in violence on record.[11] Swastikas appear on college campuses and public streets, the white nationalist symbol is flashed, and cemeteries, synagogues, and mosques are vandalized. The cascade of violence has become so normal in the news cycle that numbness may be setting in.

It is, in a word, frightening these days to walk when black, worship when Jewish, fly when Muslim, work when Hispanic, and come to the United States when you are a small, small child.

The collective rise of these incidents correlates with a rise in numbers, visibility, and influence of those who are called, when viewed as separate groups, minorities. Collectively, though, people of color are nearing majority status—predicted to occur in the United States around 2045.[12] In some areas, whites are already the minority.

We see this changing demographic in photographs of national congressional representatives, at least within the Democratic Party. We see the same shift also happening in the church. People of color are far more represented than ever before as bishops, presiding bishops, rostered leaders, and speakers at official conferences and assemblies. Music and liturgy from non-Western traditions are becoming commonly integrated in public worship. Both politically and religiously, the anti-immigration rhetoric is increasingly being met with a condemnation of hate and an extension of welcome and even sanctuary. While this transformation is a harbinger of hope and new possibilities for many, for those who have lost or will be losing positions of power and privilege (particularly whites), the demographic change represents a loss of culture, language, and power, all of which fuel the hate with increasing intensity and regularity.

Christians can repent of their racist and privileged history and redefine their future in myriad ways: initiating conversations about declaring a congregation to be a sanctuary, delving into the long scriptural history about welcome to the foreigner, organizing trips to the border to protect and advocate for those coming across, preaching and teaching on the troublesome texts about Jews, discovering our religious connections to Jews and

Muslims, initiating shared events with members of both communities, learning about racial disparities in one's own contexts, teaching about the long history of racial injustice from the perspective of black experience, and reconsidering the expanding references primarily to white Christian theologians and saints and white pictures of Jesus and manger scenes adorning church walls and windows.

Today, the church is poised to recognize that in this new moment of reform, we are called to reject xenophobia, racism, and anti-immigration rhetoric in all of their forms, and to see that we are all justified, declared worthy in God's sight, and therefore worthy of hospitality, welcome, safety, and justice.

Nationalism and Christian Nationalism

The terrorist attacks of September 11, 2001, were carried out by Muslim extremists disgusted with US culture and policies. That act of retributive hate, however, only fueled new waves of white extremism and far-right nationalism. That the president elected in 2012 was named Barack Hussein Obama also galvanized right-wing nationalists and white-power extremists. His victory, coupled with the increased power and presence of the internet, created an intense vortex of hate, religious bigotry, lust for revenge, and power. It is the height of irony that in the United States since 9/11, white and far-right extremists have committed more murders than any other group of domestic terrorists.[13]

Social psychologist Jonathan Haidt (1963–) makes the case that 2016 marked the year when nationalism flourished not only on US soil, but globally as well: Trump became the Republican nominee, Austria almost elected right-wing Norbert Hofer, British Parliament member Jo Cox was murdered by a man yelling "Britain first!" and Britain voted to exit the European Union. The marked rise of nationalism seems to coincide with and be tied to the rise of globalism, a political perspective that is quite comfortable with integrating cultures and races rather than assimilating them. In contrast to nationalism, globalism is inclined to welcome immigrants and policies that support safe and fair immigration. Globalists tend to engage willingly in international agreements, even ones that work against one's own national interests in favor of the global good.

No globalist principle sits well with a nationalist, of course, and it was the nationalists—especially the Christian nationalists—who tipped the scale in the 2016 presidential election.[14] One can make the case, as does religion reporter Jack Jenkins,[15] that the United States was built by way of Christian nationalism: the early settlers believed that the discovery and the growth of this nation was ordained by God, and that conviction was baked into our sense of blessed and divine destiny, one that was, by definition, white.

In fact, New York Times columnist Niraj Chokshi did a sweep of 2016 election data and discovered that neither income nor gender was the clearest indicator of whether someone supported Trump: rather, fear of globalism, the threatened loss of white identity, and the clearly detectable waning commitment to the Christian tradition flipped their switch to Trump.[16] Relatedly, sociologist Andrew Whitehead created an index to evaluate the relationship between one's commitment to nationalism and one's commitment to Trump. "For every unit increase on the Christian nationalism scale," says Whitehead, "the odds of voting for Trump increased by seven percent."[17]

It seems that Christian nationalists connected the dots between President Obama, immigration, and equal recognition of and respect for various religious traditions outside of Christianity. This perceived line did not square with their faith or patriotism, for they perceived that if followed, both God's ordination of the supremacy of the white-identified United States and God's ordination of Christianity as the One True Faith would be threatened. Taken together, Christian nationalists could see their presumption of divine right and power slipping away.

However, perceptions of their race, their religion, their country, and their privilege have been defined by a conviction that God has uniquely selected each as a quintessential and exclusive beacon of divine blessing. It should be noted that God does not object to variation, uniqueness, and patriotism, but God does object to illusions of supremacism due to any of these expressions.

In these times, Christians can be reminded that God called creation *tov* (good)—*tov meod* (very good), as a matter of fact. Our allegiance to the God who delightedly created all people and all places supersedes our allegiance to one people and one place. Given the nationalistic climate of the day and the according stakes, we are being called to commit to repudiating nationalism, most especially that which bears the name of Christian. Engaging in conversation about the competing and complementary claims of patriotism and faith, delving into the studies of biblical texts concerning the role of nations (such as Old Testament texts that reveal God working through nations outside of Israel, and Matthew 25), providing safe space to lift up what is "trimmed to the white light" in our land, participating in discussions that ask the tough questions about whether the United States is indeed more blessed by God than others, and even asking hard questions about the appropriateness of hanging any nation's flag in a Christian sanctuary where we come to worship the God of all nations—each activity can in its own way initiate a reformation of our awareness of, toleration of, implicit endorsement of, or rejection of the blight of Christian nationalism. Now is the moment to reform just that—our engagement, or lack thereof, of Christian nationalism—but to remind ourselves that Christ eliminated east, west, Jew, Greek, enslaved, free, male, and female, and to be convinced that we are all justified, all worthy in God's sight, and therefore all worthy of justice.

> We are all justified, all worthy in God's sight, and therefore all worthy of justice.

Evangelical Christianity, the Nones, and Progressive Christians

A clear line seems to link Christian nationalists and Christian evangelicals. Quite surprisingly, Christian evangelicals draw a line quite quickly and clearly from God to Trump, a man twice divorced, unfaithful to his wives, prone to bullying, and who carries an agenda that seems to fall far from Jesus's concern for the poor. However, the evangelical support for Trump easily looks past these histories because of two primary things. First, Trump's promise to quash abortion rights. This policy commitment, one that Trump has surely begun to fulfill by way of stacking the courts, is to many the key metric by which to evaluate his political worth. Indeed, it is itself worth sacrificing any other political or moral tenet. The second rationale is the belief that Trump is a modern-day Cyrus, the Persian leader who defeated the ancient Babylonians and allowed the exiled Jewish people to return to Judah. Much as they see Cyrus as having carried out God's plans despite not being Jewish, many evangelicals regard Trump as a man chosen by God to advance God's work, despite (as some of them acknowledge) the signs that Trump is far from being what they might call a "man of God."

But evangelicals are no longer the only group with religious identities—or lack of them—to hold influence in culture, politics, and policies these days. The Nones, for example, are a relatively new classification of people with nuanced religious belief, and their numbers are gaining. It's a word you almost have to see the first time to understand what is being said: in "the Nones and the church," the word *Nones* sounds like "nuns!" But it's an umbrella category for people who never attended church, who once did but no longer do, or who are not religious as traditionally defined, though they may profess belief in some form of God.

Those who have left organized religion often did so less because they disbelieved in a traditional notion of God and more because they were either dismayed by their experience of some traditional religious social doctrines (sometimes teachings against homosexuality and abortion), by the church's *lack* of social doctrines (about poverty and matters of privilege, for example), and by the church's perceived default close alignment with right-wing and conservative agendas. They also experience the church's message as having little relevance for day-to-day lives. They see the substance of the church's focus as either tone-deaf to their realities or resonant far more with a day gone past.

The Nones, a halfway point, one could say, between atheism and religiosity, are increasing both in number and in social recognition. Nones are not necessarily agnostics but instead are open to faith, albeit not as expressed in traditional ways, either individually or institutionally. Although their voting rates are lower than for other groupings, when they vote, they vote heavily Democratic.

Into this societal and religious mix come the progressive religious, a wing of religious faith that has until recently been somewhat quiet—or overlooked, depending on one's perspective. Increasingly, this group is not just publicly visible but a politically viable force. Their to-the-left movement is not at all restricted by any denomination or faith tradition, and it is claiming its place behind the pulpit and in the streets. Progressive religious leaders are becoming bolder about making political connections between Scripture, religious tradition, and contemporary politics and policies. Progressive laity are becoming bolder both about announcing their political persuasions as shaped by their religious ones and about engaging in political action precisely because of their faith. Progressive politicians are referencing their own faith and wielding the rhetorical flourishes of preachers, something we are used to hearing from either white evangelical and Republican politicians or black politicians and leaders—the likes of Martin Luther King Jr. or Jesse Jackson, themselves also preachers by training and call. In 2018, Senators Cory Booker and Elizabeth Warren were even invited guests at the interdenominational Festival of Homiletics. These are arenas and skills and commitments with which the religious right has long been familiar and adept, but to see it from the religious left is a new phenomenon and a significantly new and influential development in the world of politics and faith.[18]

It is often said that the two topics to avoid at the dinner table are religion and politics; people in these three movements—evangelical Christians, the Nones, and progressive Christians—might make that increasingly difficult to do. There is fear within each of these groups, but stemming from different worries: fear of losing religious political sway, fear of no religious political engagement, and fear of ceding religious political influence.

Now is the moment to reform our understandings of the relationship between religion and politics, prophetic and pastoral callings, what right and left mean when applied to religious persuasions, and how we define what we are called to do, not due to political or national identifications, but through the lens of our faith. Because we are all justified, worthy in God's sight, we are all worthy of justice.

Gun Violence

We can rattle off the locations of mass shootings—Columbine, Las Vegas, Orlando, Sandy Hook, Parkland, Tree of Life (we can almost be assured that there will be more by the time this book is published)—but as a society, it seems we are less and less rattled *by* these attacks. Depending on one's perspective, the debate is either about gun violence or gun rights. We cannot deny that mass shootings and gun violence are indeed on the rise. It is almost too much to imagine that debate remains about whether those statistics and the suffering behind them are acceptable by-products of the right to bear arms. What is not debated is whether massacres due to gun violence have become a normal element of US life, rued by many but tolerated by too many as the cost for the privilege of living in a land where a particular understanding of the Second Amendment holds sway. According to the *New York Times*, which references the Center for Disease Control and Prevention, 39,773 deaths occurred due to gun violence in 2017. All but a third of that number were by suicide; the rest were due to mass shootings and accidental firings.[19]

Despite these statistics, when the discussion is framed as a matter of gun rights, it often turns to a discussion, and even a defense, of what it is to be an American. Those who support fewer gun laws believe that the Second Amendment, which provides for "the right to bear arms," is inextricably related to American history and American identity. Those who support more restrictive gun laws say there is nothing more American than freedom, especially the freedom to live and go to school, a concert, or a bar without fear of being shot. It is nigh impossible, then, to separate the gun issue from a particular understanding about what it means to be a patriot. Palpable fear exists on both sides. Oddly, each group appears to be concerned about the same thing: having the right to be safe.

Now is the moment in the life of the church to enter the gun debate so that it considers the issues of greed, fear, and economic, racial, and gender violence and inequity that course through the rise in gun injuries and deaths. This participation in the debate can pose questions about God's love of life, God's grief at the loss of it, and, given our knowledge of both, what role weaponry has outside of hunting and military use. We can reflect on how to view the Second Amendment and recognize that God calls us to love, respect, and care for our neighbors. Since all are justified, worthy in God's sight, how will we live lives worthy of justice—and justice defined by whom?

Apathy

Dean Stroud tells of an essay written in 1937:

> The writer compares living in Nazi Germany to being a passenger on a train who is unaware that a bridge is being rebuilt—little by little and piece by piece—until it is no longer the old bridge but a completely new one. Only the most observant passenger traveling across the bridge every day would notice that a total transformation had occurred. In the weeks and months of those

first two years of the Third Reich, the National Socialists were slowly transforming Germany from a democratic society (*Rechtsstaat*) into a terror state (*Terrorstaat*).[20]

For us, too, the present state of things may have seemed to happen overnight. But it didn't. The factors described in the pages of this chapter—distressing, depressing, and discouraging in different ways—have been brewing, one can argue, since before the dawn of our nation. But one more factor, especially apparent when studying the state of voting habits in this nation, concerns an unwillingness to engage. We also can call this condition apathy. Apathetic people are uninterested in the process of government, perhaps because they don't understand why it matters or (to hearken to Niemöller's famous observation) because the powers that be haven't yet come for them.

Dictators and demagogues like unengaged citizens.

Dictators and demagogues like unengaged citizens. They thrive when people are not paying attention to what is going on when they aren't looking. German theologian Dorothee Sölle (1929–2003) saw the effects of apathy and was both fascinated and distressed by its pervasiveness in Germany in the days before and during World War II:

> Apathy is a form of the inability to suffer. It is understood as a social condition in which people are so dominated by the goal of avoiding suffering that it becomes a goal to avoid human relationships and contacts altogether. In so

far as the experiences of suffering, the *pathai* (Greek for the things that happen to a person, misfortunes) of life are repressed, there is a corresponding disappearance of passion for life and of the strength and intensity of its joys. . . . This doesn't mean that apathetic people . . . don't suffer—let alone that they are happy. What they lack is an awareness of their own suffering and a sensitivity for the suffering of others. They experience suffering, but they "put up with it," it doesn't move them. They have no language or gestures with which to battle suffering. Nothing is changed; they learn nothing from it.[21]

All of these years later and across the ocean, Sölle still has a point.

Marketers of any number of lifestyle products are thankful that she does. Think of all the modern companies that create gadgets and tools to which we pay indulgences, seeking to justify ourselves with the added bonus of insulating ourselves from suffering. On social media, many people post cute dog memes and cute sayings and recipes but nary a single status update concerning matters of public policy, public outrage, or protest about the treatment of the "least of these."

Embedded in Sölle's observation about apathy is a critique of the church. Trump was elected in large part because the church has been too terrified to speak up against him and the sentiments he both represented and fomented. We have feared suffering by fearing conflict, fearing loss of members, and fearing the line between church and state. At least at the congregational level, we have been selectively apathetic and deeply invested in preserving our own well-being while showing less concern for preserving the well-being of others who have been marginalized, disenfranchised, threatened, and oppressed.

Scripture, of course, is filled with politics: politics affecting faith, and faith affecting politics; politicians affecting the faithful, and the faithful affecting politicians. Now is the moment for Christians, in the name of our faith, to reform our engagement—or lack of the same—in politics. Reminding ourselves through proclamation and Bible study of the long scriptural heritage of the deep intersection between our allegiance to God and our participation in God's world would transform apathy into compassion, reticence into willingness, quietude into clamors for justice. For, in fact, all are justified, declared worthy in God's sight, and therefore worthy of justice.

Standing against Fear

We live in a moment saturated with tremendous and widespread fear, infusing all of the issues named in this chapter. Scripture reminds us time and again that we are not to be afraid, but it does not say we have nothing to fear. And as a culture, we are afraid. Not coincidentally, we are also angry. In fact, the word *anxiety* comes from the Latin *anxietatem*, meaning anguished and troubled. It is directly related to the word *anger*, which comes from the Latin *angere*, which means, quite literally, to torment, to tighten, to squeeze, and to *anguish*, which comes from *angustia*—no surprise here that *angustia* means a choking sensation, or distress, or even rage. The two are related not just in life but in word history.

Fear yields anger. Anger yields more fear, and the cycle begins again. For example, those who receive their livelihood from fossil fuels, ranching, hog farming, logging, and making fertilizers or pesticides (to mention just a few) have good reason to fear changes that might affect their ability to make a living from these activities and products. Those who look at the statistics about global warming and who ponder the environmental, economic, political, cultural, and health consequences associated with it have good reason to be afraid about what will happen if nothing changes.

In 2008, Bill Bishop (1953–) wrote a revolutionary book called *The Big Sort*, which details how US citizens have clustered themselves by way of neighborhood, vocation, churches, and news sources. We hear not only what we like to hear, but all that we can hear. Anything that seems to cast doubt on our framework becomes suspect—fake, even. We fear being wrong, fear having to admit that we were wrong, fear new ways of thinking, and fear that new ways of thinking will change our minds.[22]

Palpable fear and anxiety are everywhere. But there are ways to overcome, and every now and again, we can see indications that some resistance to and rejection of the fear is occurring. Occasionally, fear seems to be reduced, to be pushed back, to dissipate. One of the tragic shootings, for example—the one that took place in Parkland, Florida—changed the conversation. The students and their families accepted thoughts and prayers, but they didn't stop there. They transformed their grief and fear into action, which has begun to change the conversation, change hearts, and change minds. Moreover, these young people are making a case that they can change the world and can do so with nothing more complicated than a ballot and an occasional March for Our Lives in Washington, DC. If they can do it, wounded and grieving and angry as they are, they are asking us to consider whether all of us might opt for hope and life and change.

"Do not be afraid." If only it were easy. We are afraid. It does no good to pretend we aren't or to gloss over that we are. But we must not let fear lead to despair. We are being called to avoid the trap of trusting our fear more than we trust our hope in the resurrection. We are all children of God, all recipients of grace, all justified, and all worthy of justice. This new Reformation comes, then, even as we are called to say that fear is real. Death is real. We are to call these things what they are. But justice, love, and life are realer even now, right this very moment. By the grace of God, we can call these things into being.

> We need to avoid the trap of trusting our fear more than we trust our hope in the resurrection.

Time and again, Scripture also reminds us to trust God, because we have any number of other gods clamoring for our trust. *Trust* also has a word history, one tied to the same root (**deru*) from which we get tree; it means to remain strong and steadfast, and it now is related to the German *Trost*, which means to comfort, soothe, console.

Whether we are small children afraid of the monster in the closet in the dark of the night or fearful full-grown adults tempted to or yearning to closet off the tumult of the world, we are now in a moment in which we are called to trust not our fears, nor the good reasons for our fears, but rather to trust in God. We are being called to be reminded that this is the God who calls hope out of despair, calm out of chaos, and life out of death.

We are being called to notice what is penultimate and what is ultimate—what is not worthy of our trust and what is.

We are being called to recall that we are all justified, declared worthy in God's sight, and by the grace of this same God, therefore worthy of justice.

Discussion Questions

1. The author briefly describes the major five-hundred-year epochs of Christian history through the lens of Phyllis Tickle, who calls our present age "the Great Emergence." Where does the author suggest our new era of the church will or should take us? Where do you see the church and the Christian faith going as you look ahead?

2. On pages 122–52, the author addresses several factors or forces in our current age that serve as both challenges and opportunities for people of faith. For you, what rings most true about these forces or factors? With what perspectives do you disagree? Why?

3. In your mind, which of the factors or forces listed on pages 122–52 are most pressing? Why? As a person of faith, how can you imagine addressing this factor or force in tangible ways?

4. Fear and anger are by-products of uncertainty and change. What fears do you have for yourself, our society, or the church? What, if anything, makes you angry? What words of direction or comfort do you find in the author's words?

6

Here We Imagine

In January 2006, on her Peabody Award winning public radio show *On Being*, Krista Tippett broadcast her interview with Dr. Esther Sternberg, research director at the Arizona Center for Integrative Medicine at the University of Arizona. Dr. Sternberg is powerfully curious about studying emotional stress by engaging research from the fields of study concerning the central nervous system and the immune system. She wants to know what causes stress, why some people suffer from it more than others, how it affects our physical well-being, and whether we can reduce its presence and its effects in our lives.

It wasn't until the 1950s, she said in the interview with Tippett, that the term *stress* was coined by physiologist Hans Selye. At that time, technologies offering the ability to measure physiological responses started to come into their own in his field. Selye realized that when the body is stressed, the hormonal and vascular reactions mirrored outputs seen when physical pressures were measured in the worlds of engineering and physics. So he adopted the word *stress* from these fields and adapted it for his own application. In fact, Sternberg noted, Selye went around the globe trying to get that word, that very word, into the languages of every dictionary in the world. Tippett and Sternberg even mentioned that Germans talk about being *gestressed* and that something is very *stressig*, all due to Selye's efforts long ago.

In her interview, Sternberg also discussed ideas about the causes of stress. Even prior to Selye's adoption of the term, she said, five causes of "modern" stress were noted in 1880: "the periodical press, the telegraph, the steam railroads, the sciences, and . . . the mental activity of women." Yes, the mental activity of women! But as Dr. Sternberg noted, what was really being described was the effects of the Industrial Revolution. And she added this explanation:

> Now, but why is it these things are stressful? Because change, novelty, is one of the most potent triggers of the stress response. And that's a good thing, because when an animal finds itself in a new environment, [such as] if a field mouse wanders into a new field, if it didn't have a stress response, if it wouldn't suddenly sit up and look around and become vigilant and focused and ready to fight or flee, if it just went to sleep, it would get eaten by the next cat that came along. Right?
>
> So you need your stress response to survive. And novelty must, therefore, trigger the stress response. So the problem happens when the stress response goes on too long, when it's active when it shouldn't be active, when you're pumping out these hormones and nerve chemicals

at max. And that's when you get sick, and that's when these chemicals and hormones have an effect on the immune system and change its ability to fight disease.[1]

One hundred fifty years after the Industrial Revolution, change, albeit of a different kind, is undoubtedly upon us, and people are *gestressed.* As a culture, we are overwhelmed, angry, distrustful, and fearful, and one could easily argue that we are collectively sick. We are neither healthy, nor healed, nor whole. We need *soteria.* We need salvation.

We might also need sabbath. Darby Kathleen Ray (1964–), who is associate professor of religious studies and the director of the Faith and Work Initiative at Millsaps College in Jackson, Mississippi, writes eloquently about the need to rest:

> To live deeply requires rest and reflection. Occasional binges of inactivity or vacation—mere crisis management—will not suffice . . . Sabbath practices . . . summon us to "become attuned to *holiness in time*" (says Abraham Heschel). Sabbath . . . connects us to "what is eternal in time." It summons us "to turn from the results of creation to the mystery of creation. . . ."

When the nourishing rest of sabbath time becomes the foundation for our work in the world, that work holds new promise. It is not that the daily grind disappears or that systems of injustice are suddenly transformed. The desire for work that is personally meaningful, socially valued, and adequately compensated remains unfulfilled for most people, which means the struggle to rethink work and its defining systems must go on. And yet, despite these sad realities, rested work—work as it is viewed from the standpoint of rest, and work that is nourished by deep rest—gestures in significant ways toward transformation.[2]

Ray encourages readers—especially those inclined to feel overwhelmed by the world's pressing issues—to find and offer salvation in Jesus's name by resting, not in order to retreat from the needs of this world but precisely to recharge for the needs of this world. Given the overwhelming number and nature of claims and calls and cries offered by creatures and creation alike, it is easy to forget or discount that we are finite and that there is not one thing we can do about that. We are finite, and alone we cannot save the world, save our nation, save the church, save our congregation, save our families, or save ourselves. We are finite, and alone we cannot stop all the lies, stop the hate, stop the violence. We are bound, and we are bounded by our finitude and, to a degree, by the finitude of possibilities we can see in this moment.

There is innate frustration within that truth, but there is also innate grace. We cannot do it all. We can't. We are, as Luther so rightly pointed out long ago, justified because and even so. So then, after the relief of that obvious but overlooked truth settles in and settles us down, come at least two responses:

1. How do we tend to ourselves and cope with the loss and frustration of what we can't do?
2. How can we tend to others who are parched, dry, and brittle?

Rest, Restore, Celebrate

Ever so conveniently, the words *rest* and *restore* come from the same word as *restaurant*. In fact, the Frenchman who came up with the word *restaurant* had a soup shop that was so good he promised it would "restore" the spirits of all who slurped his soup. He was so convinced of it that he, a Monsieur Boulanger, had a conflated Latin version of Matthew 11:28 inscribed above his store's window: "Come to me, all who labor, and I will give you rest." The word *rest* in Latin is *restaurabo*.

As "people of the banquet," I think we can work with that. We are all yearning to be restored, that is, to be fed. Not only are we stressed; we also are hungry—hungry for rest, hungry for calm, hungry for justice, hungry for kindness, hungry for grace, hungry for peace, hungry for hope. The church is called to feed, and people, both within and outside it, yearn to be fed, yearn to be restored, yearn to come to the restaurant.

> The church is called to feed, and people, both within and outside it, yearn to be fed, yearn to be restored.

This moment, then, paradoxically calls us to rest. It also calls us to cultivate, celebrate, and give thanks for beauty. Twenty years back, two dear friends of mine, who both have since died, were generous beyond measure. They lived off of one salary and gave away the other salary to organizations they felt reflected God's agenda for the world: a seminary, a public radio station, a nonprofit, a political party. And the spare bedroom in their basement always seemed to be occupied. They made sure someone always was staying in it. It made no sense to them to have a spare bed in need of a person when people were desperately in need of a bed! In addition, they had a habit of buying four season tickets to the local symphony. For each concert, they invited two people to join them as guests—first at my friends' home for appetizers and cocktails, then for dinner at one of the finest restaurants in town, and then off to the symphony. My friends were convinced that donating money and housing to people exemplifies the reign of God, but so, too, does sharing good beverages, good food, and good music. In this time of anxiety, anger, and stress, their way of life is good counsel for our time of life: celebrate, savor, and serve. Joy itself is an act of resistance.

Imagine

Luther was gifted with a vivid imagination. Despite the heft of the ecclesial, theological, political, and cultural traditions in play, the man named something that wasn't yet, and by doing so, he called something new into being. His imagination, his capacity to see things as they were *and* as they could be, called the Reformation into being.

I accidentally noticed the correlation between imagination and reformation thanks to a research habit of mine: I tag every quote and bit of information I find. For example, if I want to find all the occasions when my research mentions "reform," I can scroll down my tag list and click on all of the sources. But tags also help me discover connections or reveal insights that I might have otherwise missed, thanks to the other tags also associated with the same research. A scroll through the tags revealed that imagination is not just a precursor but a necessary component of reformation. And under tags for both "reformation" and "imagination," no scholar's name kept popping up more than Old Testament theologian Walter Brueggemann (1933–). There is much about this world that he would like to reform, and he has an expansive imagination. He is convinced that God does, too.

God is not cemented into place, Brueggemann teaches; God is not prefabbed and is not immutable. Instead, God is creative and "imaginative." As Bruggemann puts it, "God is still operative and exercises choices along the way; . . . the world is still open and we are not fated; . . . human agents, as creatures in God's image, share in God's imaging activity."[3] Deftly, Brueggemann makes the direct connection that if we have been created in God's image (*imago Dei*), we share in God's imagining activity. We imagine God. It's all the more clear in this passage from him: "The ones who minister to the imagination, who enable people to see the world differently and to live now in the world they see are fatally dangerous to the establishment."[4]

> When we unite our imagination with God's image, present realities are not just challenged, but upended.

The people to whom he is referring, of course, are religious leaders and worshippers who gather as and constitute the community of Christ and proclaim its witness. When we unite our imagination with God's image, present realities are not just challenged, but upended. Reformations of both church and society take place.

Imagining the Future in the Present

To imagination we add a word mentioned earlier: *prolepsis*, which is the act of bringing the eschaton, those new days, into the present. Literally, it means "the taking beforehand." The eschaton is not here, but it is promised—and it is imagined.

Just as our lives are shaped and changed by the promise of a lunch date or a wedding date, so too are our lives as Christians shaped and changed by the promise of resurrection. Death—of any sort and form—doesn't win. And prolepsis has everything to do with imagination, as the late Presbyterian theologian Eugene Peterson (1932–2018) sketches out:

> We who are made in the *"image"* of God have, as a consequence, *imag*-ination. Imagination is the capacity to make connections between the visible and the invisible, between heaven and earth, between present and past, between present and future. For Christians, whose largest investment is in the invisible, the imagination is indispensable, for it is only by means of the imagination that we can see reality whole, in context.[5]

By trusting and having faith in the eschatological future and striving to align it with the present moment, we can engage the future proleptically.

My late mentor Walter Bouman used to explain proleptic eschatology with the help of a distressing quirk: Walt read the last chapter first in his mystery novels. He justified himself (pun intended) by saying that in doing so, he entered into the story differently. He knew that the attic door was fine to open but the closet door was not. He knew that the woman in the red dress could be trusted but the man in blue jeans could not. He knew whether the book was worth the read. And he knew how it was going to end. In the same way, he said (still justifying this head-shaking habit), as Christians, we have read the last chapter. We know how the book ends. We know that life wins. We know, then, that even though we are afraid, we have nothing to fear, ultimately. We know that fear and tears and death do not win the day. And we know what sort of life is promised, because we know the ways of the one who was raised.

Proleptic eschatology is not a term that Christians use much—if at all. It is certainly not one commonly used in public discourse! But for Christians, the moment has come to dream upon this concept as we consider policies, politics, and the politicians whom we elect.

Under the rubric of the separation of church and state, some might bristle at the idea that faith can and should influence politics. But it is really a matter of religious fidelity and alignment: being trimmed, that is, to God means that all that we do and say is aligned with God's vision and agenda. If we make decisions trimmed to another god, then we are out of alignment—not *tzadek*, not righteous. The late Rev. Dr. James Cone put it like this:

What is the Christian faith, and what does it have to say about the rich and the poor and the social, economic, and political conditions that determine their relationship? To answer this question is not easy in North America, because we live in a society that claims to separate church and state, religion and politics. "Christianity," it is often said, "is concerned with spiritual reality but not with the material conditions of people." If the Christian faith is no more than the cultural and political interests of the rules transformed into theological categories, then Karl Marx is right in his contention that religion is the opium of the people and therefore should be eliminated along with other legitimizing agencies in an oppressive society. But if religion generally and the Christian faith in particular is an imaginative and apocalyptic vision about the creation of a new humanity that is derived from the historical and political struggles of oppressed peoples, then to describe it as a sedative is to misunderstand religion's essential nature and its latent revolutionary and humanizing thrust in society.[6]

The church is comprised of an entire people claimed by an imaginative and apocalyptic vision! And when it doesn't engage this same imaginative and apocalyptic vision, the church compromises an entire people and the faith they purport to have. This vision is eschatological, proleptic, revolutionary, and reformative, and moves us to engage in concern for the "least of these." That is constitutive of who we are and constitutes what we do. Any finger pointed to the separation of church and state, Cone says, is one pointing away from the poor. Now, some insist that there should be a strict separation between church and state, and between the Kingdom on the Left and the Kingdom on the Right (not to be confused with the right and left of today's political and religious jargon!). They are of the firm opinion that the church is to have nothing to do with politics, not even by way of advocacy. This severance should hold true, they assert, regardless of whether we are speaking of the church proper or of individual people of faith. In fact, many believe that the church is legally prevented from social-justice engagement. But a review of the US origins of the notion found in the Bill of Rights regarding the separation between religion and politics reveals that a significant misunderstanding has happened along the way. In fact, the intention to which the First Amendment refers was rather to protect religion from the state, rather than vice versa! We get a good whiff of what the framers had in mind when we peek at the 1786 Virginia Statute for Religious Freedom:

> No man shall be compelled to frequent or support any religious worship, place, or ministry whatsoever, nor shall be enforced, restrained, molested, or burthened [sic] in his body or goods, nor shall otherwise suffer on account of his religious opinions or belief; but that all men shall be free to profess, and by argument to maintain, their opinions in matters of Religion, and that the same shall in no wise diminish, enlarge, or affect their civil capacities.[7]

Here, the seeds of what eventually became understood as "the separation of church and state" are planted: one's religious belief may not be regulated by the government. Eventually, this notion of the distinct roles of church and state grew and bloomed into the Constitution twice. First, Article VI states that "no religious Test shall ever be required as a Qualification to any Office or public Trust under the United States." And second, the First Amendment reads, "Congress shall make no law respecting an establishment of religion, or prohibiting the free exercise thereof; or abridging the freedom of speech, or of the press; or the right of the people peaceably to assemble, and to petition the Government for a redress of grievances."

It's worth noting that the phrase "separation of church and state" is not found in either of these constitutional references. It is, however, discoverable in a letter from Thomas Jefferson in 1802 to the Danbury Baptist Association in Connecticut: "I contemplate with sovereign reverence that act of the whole American people which declared that their legislature should 'make no law respecting an establishment of religion, or prohibiting the free exercise thereof,' thus building a wall of separation between Church & State."[8] In short, all of these references, extra-constitutional and constitutional alike, essentially seek to prevent the Diet of Worms happening here: the government may not dictate what someone should believe, practice, or teach.

It is true that certain Internal Revenue Service regulations dictate whether or not churches as churches may *lobby* for a *candidate*.[9] Such actions are not permissible—although open candidate forums and debates are. Additionally, the IRS is concerned about the proportionate amount of time churches spend on advocacy for specific issues; among other matters, the IRS wants to ensure that churches are not lobbying organizations cloaked as nonprofits. To that degree, there are some general guidelines about the percentage of time and resources spent on advocacy. Because context and call vary from congregation to congregation, the specific restrictions are determined on a case-by-case basis. But insofar as churches preach and act in a manner consistent with their theology, drawing direct connections between their social advocacy and their faith tenets, as the apostle Paul would say, "There is no law against such things" (Gal 5:23). In fact, given our holy texts, it is impossible to *not* make claims about issues of social justice, for concern about the poor, the homeless, the foreigners, the sick, and the care of creation is laced throughout our Scriptures.

Now, in this new time, the church is being asked to recall that the gospel is addressed to the plural. Jesus isn't risen just for you. And Jesus isn't risen just for me. Jesus is risen for the sake of the world. The world needs the gospel, because everywhere in the world, life is being threatened. All the recent climate science tells us that, in fact, the life *of the world* is being threatened! This is the precise point that Luther missed, and I believe much of the theological tradition that followed him did, too. A basic theme of both the Old and New Testaments that is lifted up time and time again is liberation from death for all people *in the now.* Not later. We are not intended to wait for liberation to come about

> The world needs the gospel, because everywhere in the world, life is being threatened.

after we all die. Jesus came so that we can have life and have it abundantly *now*. As collective bearers of his name, the Christian church is now called to bear his gospel to the world.

Luther's latently conveyed belief in natural law as evidence of God's will, his focus on individual forgiveness, and our misunderstanding of what is and is not permissible for church engagement under the law have powerfully affected the willingness of the church to be engaged in rejecting death as it is found in cultural, economic, and political systems. The early church, though, got it. We see it most vividly in Acts, a book that many scholars assume was written by the same author as the Gospel of Luke. Acts describes the first Christians translating the news of the risen Jesus into immediate social-economic action. In fact, Hopkins sees Acts as the very heart and the very model of Christian communal identity and communal engagement. He's convinced that, by crafting a political economy based on the needs of the "least of these," the first Christian community didn't only perceive and didn't only preach but also enacted the resurrection news. These believers grounded everything they did in their faith conviction that life is to be celebrated in worship and stewarded into the broader community. They met together, finding their identity bound up in their neighbor's needs and not their own wants. They offered, welcomed, and shared among themselves despite differences and scarcity (see Acts 2:44–47; 4:32–37). And they offered assistance to the "least of these" outside the community: "Through intense prayer, great joy, and jubilant thanksgiving, political economy incorporates celebration of communal ownership and distribution as God's blessings."[10] That's *radical* stuff—radical, of course, meaning root. That's rooted stuff, the stuff in which we are rooted: this early community sharing God's blessing by ensuring *soteria* in the now.

A New Reformation

I do believe a new Reformation is afoot. It is a Reformation of homiletic expectations, of ecclesial identity, of theological understandings, of political and social engagement, and of communal commitment. We are simply being called to put faith into action and to see that faith is deed as much as—and perhaps more than—word. As Cone writes:

> To know the truth is to do the truth. Speaking and doing are bound together so that what we say can be authenticated only by what we do. Unfortunately, the Western church has not always been clear on this point. Its mistake has often been the identification of heresy with word rather than action. By failing to explicate the connection between word and action, the church tended to identify the gospel with right speech and thus became its chief heretic. The church became so preoccupied with its own spoken word about God that it failed to hear and thus live according to God's word of freedom for the poor. From Augustine to Schleiermacher, it is hard to find a theologian in the Western church who defines the gospel in terms of God's liberation of the oppressed.
>
> The same is true in much of the contemporary speech about God. It can be seen in the separation of theology

from ethics and the absence of liberation in both. The chief mistake of contemporary white theology is not simply found in what it says about God, though that is not excluded. It is found in its separation of theory from praxis, and the absence of liberation in its analysis of the gospel.[11]

Those words both indict and liberate.

Luther might not have liked what Cone said, but he would have admired how he said it! Cone's point is that the gospel is to be proclaimed and enacted wherever death is present. In the Western church, we have tended to experience death and see it present in the passing of a loved one or in fear of our own individual sinfulness. Cone, though, shines a light on other deaths that we might not see or want to see, because they involve the deaths of our comfort, our ignorance, and our privilege.

> We incarnate what we are by definition: ambassadors of the gospel.

In point of fact, words can't help but be translated into action now, wherever life of any sort is threatened. If we proclaim, we speak of God; if we speak of God, we proclaim the gospel; if we proclaim the gospel, we preach liberation from death; and if we preach liberation from death, we notice death in more places than just the cemetery or our own private sins. We incarnate what we are by definition: ambassadors of the gospel.

What does this look like on the ground, though? What does it mean to be this sort of church? It might mean that we have to redefine church. Bouman did just that by sketching out three models of the church, adopted and adapted here. Two forms, he thought, were extant, while one was being called into being. Each form of church is detailed according to thirteen elements: its orientation, its understanding of salvation, its basic question, its understanding of doctrine, its emphasis on eschatology, its grasp of sin, its notion of temptation, its ethical framework, its understanding of church, its view of ecumenism, its posture toward social justice, its take on worship, and its perspective on evangelism.

In the following table, the first column lists these elements. The other three columns describe these elements as expressed in each model of church. For the Salvation Church, the primary focus is getting people to convert to belief in Jesus so they will get into heaven. The Service Church is mostly concerned with having high numbers in church and satisfied members (customers). The fourth column describes what I believe is the direction to which the church is being (and has been for some time) called: the Anticipatory Church. It is also closest to the church found in Acts. "Anticipatory" is the perfect name for this model, for its very name is exactly proleptic: the root words for *anticipate* mean, quite literally, to take before. Those who identify as participants in the Anticipatory Church anticipate—that is, they take before it has fully come—the reign of God in all that they do: how they worship, how they tend to one another, how they consider their role in society, how they perceive threat, and how they enact the

Model's Elements	Models[12]		
	Salvation Church	Service Church	Anticipatory Church
Primary focus	Ministry of ensuring individual salvation after death	Ministry of attending to personal, cultural, and communal needs	Ministry to the redemptive reign of God
Salvation's meaning	Means of reaching otherwordly heaven	Means of having one's needs met; personal fulfillment	The proleptic and ultimate consummation of the reign of God
Basic question	What will ensure or achieve this salvation?	What will best serve the client (customer)?	How do the church and the individual Christian witness to the reign of God?
Understanding of doctrine	Fundamentally ideological: what must be believed in order to get into heaven and not be damned to hell	Contextually, culturally bound impressions of the church's teachings	Teachings that reflect the reign of God and believers' role in it

Model's Elements	Models		
	Salvation Church	Service Church	Anticipatory Church
Eschatology	Exclusively concerns what happens after death	One doctrine among many, not essential to an understanding of Christian faith and living	A constitutive element of Christian faith and life that discerns the fulfillment of God's vision and seeks to inject it into the present
Definition of sin	Doing moral wrong, often identified as a transgression that concerns some facet of sexuality, such as homosexuality, abortion, sex outside of marriage	Having a problem or being broken; a term largely avoided within this tradition	Misdirected trust in the penultimate rather than trust in the ultimate; an action that protects the self from a perceived threat of death
Definition of temptation	Whatever tries to get one to do a moral wrong	Whatever leads to an inadequate sense of self or relationship with another	Whatever leads to violation or abandonment of the reign of God

Model's Elements	Models		
	Salvation Church	Service Church	Anticipatory Church
Primary ethical impulse	Strict adherence to God's biblical commandments	Acting in a loving way; action based on the situation (i.e., situational ethics)	Witnessing to the reign of God as primarily identified in Jesus's life, death, and resurrection
Understanding of church	The necessary means of salvation	Those served by the clergy, perceived largely as customers	The very goal and witness to the eschaton; the proleptic community of the risen Christ
Unity and ecumenism	Unity invisible; ecumenism optional	Ostensible approval of unity; pragmatic competition for "potential customers"	Each are considered goals of and witness to the eschaton; the reign of God in motion

Model's Elements	Models		
	Salvation Church	Service Church	Anticipatory Church
Role of social action	A distraction from the otherworldly attainment of salvation	Increasingly an element, but advocacy highlighted at the denominational level; philanthropic donations to various causes welcomed	Essential as a witness to the reign of God, particularly by way of drawing attention to justice, stewardship, compassion, and the pursuit of peace
Worship	Praise worship is key, the Eucharist not; baptism seen as a means to ensure entry into heaven	Whatever will get the most people into the pews; affirming of the gathered worshippers	Sacraments are foundational as initiation into and participation in the reign of God and the witness to and discipleship of that reign
Perspective on evangelism	Essential to save people from damnation	Primarily about getting more members and contributors	An invitation to participate in the eschatological vision, to be convinced that life is stronger than death

promises of God. They anticipate the reign of God in what they proclaim and in what they do.

Together these models provide an extremely helpful rubric for both personal and congregational reflection, and they invite our own self- and congregational reflection. How do *we* fill in these categories? What do our answers reveal about us and our understanding about God, our faith, and what it all means in the now?

Clearly, the thesis of this book is to urge that the church move radically to the profile of the third model. The Anticipatory Church is trimmed not to the false lights of anxiety about one's ultimate fate, nor to pleasing people and avoiding conflict, nor to protecting familiar systems. Instead, it is trimmed to the white light of the news that Jesus did not stay dead. If that is true, it is a truth revealing that God is in the business of putting death to death and replacing it with life. There is then no reason that we should fear death and remain in bondage to it. Instead, we are freed to see death where it is, to call it what it is, and to act in the name of the resurrected one to steward life there instead.

Luther's news that we are justified—there is nothing that we can or need to do to earn God's grace—is as relevant and freeing now as it was then. But his theological breakthrough needs to break through the centuries' hold it has had on the present church. There is a new context to address, one where his concern about personal salvation can actually be detrimental, not least of all to those very same people seeking personal salvation. In fact, our focus on private sinfulness has added to private and public suffering: we have lost the sense that we are participants in systems that are sinful and have lost the conviction that repentance might mean overturning those systems—even, it must be said, to our own detriment, when we are one of the privileged.

Once we begin to see that justification is intrinsically related to justice, we begin to see that confession means to name our privilege, to repent of our privilege, to abdicate our privilege, and to work toward ending systems that unfairly offer privilege to some but not to all. This is, of course, the work of proclamation; it has been said that rostered leaders are called not to serve the congregation but to serve the gospel. I am convinced that any sermon that does not mention Jesus's resurrection is, I am sure, a fine Bible study; it is not, however, proclamation. Proclamation calls us to proclaim the gospel, which is the good news, which is that Jesus is risen. We all need that news, at *least* during weekly worship, in powerful ways these days. Death is real. Life is realer. Jesus Christ ushered in life. We are Christians. We are assured of life. We are ambassadors of life wherever there is death.

That means comforting the grieving, to be sure! But it also means, where possible, preventing grief. We are called to question which policies and systems cause grief and, conversely, which most closely align with Jesus's examples of *soteria*. Matthew 25 addresses this clearly in verses 44–45: "'Lord, when was it that we saw you hungry

> Justification is intrinsically related to justice.

or thirsty or a stranger or naked or sick or in prison, and did not take care of you?' Then he will answer them, 'Truly I tell you, just as you did not do it to one of the least of these, you did not do it to me.'"

Denominations, not least of all my Evangelical Lutheran Church in America (ELCA), have been increasingly and admirably vocal and public with their advocacy and with their invitations for members to follow them in their justice pursuits. Through social statements, news alerts about troubling legislation, invitations to respond and directions for how to engage representatives, or highlighting of the inclusivity of the church, denominations are more and more on the front lines of social justice. But as mentioned earlier, it is understandably harder to encourage this sort of justice participation at the congregational level, in large part because although the corporate risks may be high, the personal ones are higher and perhaps felt more intensely. On a professional and a personal level, it is tremendously risky these days for a pastor to preach on the intersections between text and context, or to raise questions about whether present-day policies align with God's agenda. Lutheran pastors who do so, however, are living up to the promises they made regarding the expectations of proclamation and advocacy listed in the ELCA's *Vision and Expectations* for ordained ministers.[13] Faithful though such a pastor might be in serving, these expectations are less known and less welcome when they involve naming uncomfortable politics and policies.

Given that, this moment is an occasion for conferences and synods to discuss ways in which colleagues and laity can provide active support for rostered leaders, pastors, and councils who pick up this proclamatory cross and thereby run the risk of being run out of town. Collegial and corporate presence at worship services and at public meetings, as well as the creation of financial nets and networks to offer tangible support in the event one loses a call would be themselves incarnate ways of being ambassadors of the gospel, and inviting rostered leaders to serve the gospel all the more freely.

It strikes me, too, that the purported dichotomy between prophetic leadership and pastoral leadership is not only false but toxic. By "prophetic," people seem to mean harsh, bold, and divisive in speech, even if faithful. By "pastoral," people seem to mean nice, nonconflictual, and welcoming to all. But the pastoral is the prophetic, and the prophetic is the pastoral. If one expands the notion of sin to include even our inadvertent participation in systemic evils, such as racism, sexism, global warming, and (one could argue) even capitalism, we can't help but name it as sin as confidently as we do the more commonly accepted sins, for many of which repentance requires no change in our lifestyles and voting habits. Regardless of the nature of the sin, we are in bondage to it and are called to welcome the proclamation that frees us from it.

Last, in these days of strife and stress and suspicion, it would do communities well to engage in habits of joy. Music, feasts, art, dance, heritage celebrations, and contemplative beauty fling open doors to remind us that the world is indeed *tov* (and in fact *tov meod*) create bonds, stave off despair, and are themselves welcome resurrection-in-motion.

So I return to my earlier theme: *the first commandment matters*. Who or what is our ultimate God? On what basis do we make that claim? What difference does that allegiance make in our actions—the way we treat the stranger, the lover, the friend, the enemy, the child, the non-Christian, the undocumented, the poor, the wealthy, the earth? And how does this affect the way we eat, the way we drive, the way we purchase, and the way we vote? The answer is: in every possible way.

Our God is revealed in every move we make, and people are watching. Some are waiting. Some are wondering, What is the Christian God, and how is that God seen in Christian living? Our God, of course, is the one revealed in the risen Jesus. Jesus came and lived among us, not just to talk about the reign of God but to enact it. Insofar as we call ourselves Christians, we believe that the resurrection confirmed Jesus as the Messiah, and we are called to enact this same reign. We are being called *now* to see death not just in our sinfulness, but wherever there is a threat to life.

> Our God is revealed in every move we make, and people are watching.

My father is a retired preacher, and a retired righteous preacher at that. Decades ago, he wrote a sermon that still has traction. It was so moving that an artist in the congregation, created from it a lithograph, lifting some of the words of his text, words that now hang above my living room couch. The words are a benediction to the advent of this new Reformation moment:

Shalom is a word that is broad in the extreme. It has to do with wholeness, with fulfillment.

Shalom paints a vision of the way things will one day be with all hands helping.

Shalom knows of a lion lying down with a lamb, of the thirsty having drink, hungry having food, naked being clothed.

Shalom knows of swords being beaten into plowshares, of justice and freedom.

Shalom knows of strangers being welcomed, the sick and imprisoned being visited.

Shalom knows of sorrow and tears disappearing and death being no more.

Shalom has as its agenda liberation and reconciliation.

Shalom has as its agenda love, hope, and renewal.

Shalom has as its agenda drought and famine.

Shalom has as its agenda war and hatred.

Shalom has as its agenda prejudice and oppression.

Shalom has as its agenda sickness and suffering.

We are not bound by our own lives, our own deaths, but live within the great parentheses of Shalom.

Shalom is the shape of the future, the vision of that to which a mysterious power summons us all here and now, in the role of servant, in bringing and establishing justice and freedom, grace and peace.

Discussion Questions

1. Do you agree or disagree with the author that we live in a stressful (*gestressed*) time? If you agree, what do you think is causing this stress?
2. How does the author suggest that sabbath time could help? What is the purpose of sabbath time?
3. How does the author draw a connection between reformation and imagination? What do you think of her persective?
4. The author speaks of the need for Christians to have a "proleptic" view, meaning we recognize the promise of God's redeemed future and bring it into the present. How do you understand what this means? Why is it important?
5. How would you briefly summarize the author's view of a "new Reformation moment"?
6. As you review the church types and their elements in the table on pages 176–79, what rings true in your experience? What questions or additional thoughts does the table raise? Do you recognize your own congregation or faith community in the descriptions?
7. If you believe, as the author does, that Christians are facing a new "here we stand" moment, what do you think the church today should stand for and against?
8. As you look back over your reading and discussion of this book, what new learning or perspectives did you gain? What questions were raised?

NOTES

CHAPTER 1: I CAN DO NO OTHER

1. Explanation of the first commandment in Martin Luther, "The Large Catechism," in *The Book of Concord*, ed. Robert Kolb and Timothy J. Wengert (Minneapolis: Fortress Press, 2000), 386.

CHAPTER 2: HERE I STAND

1. Joseph Sittler was recorded telling this story to a Mid-Atlantic Lutheran Student Movement meeting on February 26, 1977. The transcription of this recording can be found in Meta George, *Recordings of Joseph Sittler: Summaries of Audio Recordings Held in the Sittler Archives* (Chicago: Joseph Sittler Archives, Lutheran School of Theology at Chicago, 2009), 65.
2. John H. Westerhoff, *A Pilgrim People: Learning through the Church Year* (New York: Seabury, 2005).
3. For further information, see Jeffrey Owen Jones, "The Man Who Wrote the Pledge of Allegiance," *Smithsonian*, November 2003, https://tinyurl.com/y6ezbftk.
4. Tom Stoppard, *Rosencrantz and Guildenstern Are Dead* (New York: Grove, 1967), 63–64.
5. Anthony Kelly, *Eschatology and Hope* (Maryknoll, NY: Orbis, 2006), 5.

6. John Shelley, preface to *Political Theology*, by Dorothee Sölle, trans. John Shelley (Philadelphia: Fortress Press, 1974), xiv.

CHAPTER 3: HERE HE STOOD

1. Martin Luther, *Luther's Works*, ed. Jaroslav Pelikan and Helmut T. Lehmann, 55 vols. (St. Louis and Philadelphia: Concordia and Fortress Press, 1958–86), 32:112–13; hereafter cited LW.
2. Cynthia D. Moe-Lobeda, *Healing a Broken World: Globalization and God* (Minneapolis: Fortress Press, 2002), 79. Here she quotes Luther, "the Sacrament of the Body and Blood of Christ—Against the Fanatics," in *Martin Luther's Basic Theological Writings*, ed. Timothy F. Lull (Minneapolis: Fortress Press, 1989), 251.
3. Deanna A. Thompson, *Crossing the Divide: Luther, Feminism, and the Cross* (Minneapolis: Fortress Press, 2004), 19. For further reflection and expansion on the interrelationality of justification, Thompson's book is a rich treasury of insight.
4. Thompson, *Crossing the Divide*, 85, makes this case via a feminist hermeneutic.
5. "Selected Psalms II," LW 13:197.
6. See Thompson, *Crossing the Divide*, 51.
7. LW 21:116.
8. LW 45:105.
9. Thompson, *Crossing the Divide*, 51.
10. Moe-Lobeda, *Healing a Broken World*, 85–86, quoting from "Freedom of a Christian" as found in Timothy F. Lull, ed. *Martin Luther's Basic Theological Writings* (Minneapolis: Fortress Press, 1989), 625, 618, 619.
11. LW 25:285.
12. Moe-Lobeda, *Healing a Broken World*, 81, quoting from Luther's writings in Lull, *Martin Luther's Basic Theological Writings*, 331 and 619, respectively.
13. LW 21:314–15.
14. Thompson, *Crossing the Divide*, 19.
15. Thompson, *Crossing the Divide*, 10.

16. Valerie Saiving Goldstein, "The Human Situation: A Feminine View," *Journal of Religion* 40, no. 2 (April 1960): 100.
17. See Michael G. Baylor, ed., *The Radical Reformation*, Cambridge Texts in the History of Political Thought (Cambridge: Cambridge University Press, 1991), 231–38.

CHAPTER 4: HERE THEY STOOD

1. LW 24:230.
2. Martin Luther, "The Large Catechism," in *The Book of Concord*, ed. Robert Kolb and Timothy J. Wengert (Minneapolis: Fortress Press, 2000), 389.
3. Luther, "Large Catechism," 388.
4. James Cone, *Speaking the Truth: Ecumenism, Liberation, and Black Theology* (Grand Rapids: Eerdmans, 1986), 39.
5. Reggie L. Williams, *Bonhoeffer's Black Jesus: Harlem Renaissance Theology and an Ethic of Resistance* (Waco, TX: Baylor University Press, 2014), 25. Here Williams notes that he draws upon Dorothee Sölle's work *Suffering*, trans. Everett R. Kalin (Philadelphia: Fortress Press, 1975), especially pages 22–32. On these pages, Sölle sketches a tradition of God as nothing more than a "sadist" and an "executioner" (29), seen powerfully on display in the story of Abraham and Isaac. She closes the chapter by saying, "When you look at human suffering concretely you destroy all innocence, all neutrality, every attempt to say, 'It wasn't I; there was nothing I could do; I didn't know.' In the face of suffering you are either with the victim or the executioner—there is no other option. Therefore that explanation of suffering that looks away from the victim and identifies itself with a righteousness that is supposed to stand behind the suffering has already taken a step in the direction of theological sadism, which wants to understand God as the torturer" (32).
6. Williams, *Bonhoeffer's Black Jesus*, 25.

7. Dietrich Bonhoeffer, *Discipleship*, ed. Geffrey B. Kelly and John D. Godsey, trans. Reinhard Krauss and Barbara Green, Dietrich Bonhoeffer Works 4 (Minneapolis: Fortress Press, 2001), 232.

8. Williams, *Bonhoeffer's Black Jesus*, 25.

9. Cynthia D. Moe-Lobeda, *Resisting Structural Evil: Love as Ecological-Economic Vocation* (Minneapolis: Fortress Press, 2013), 59.

10. Moe-Lobeda, *Resisting Structural Evil*, 57. Anand Giridharadas, in *Winners Take All: The Elite Charade of Changing the World* (New York: Knopf, 2018), explores how extravagant philanthropy undergirds the systems that necessitate the philanthropy.

11. Erna Kim Hackett, "Why I Stopped Talking about Racial Reconciliation and Started Talking about White Supremacy," *Feisty Thoughts* (blog), August 23, 2017, https://tinyurl.com/y3nkq7t5.

12. Sandy Hotchkiss, *Why Is It Always about You? The Seven Deadly Sins of Narcissism* (New York: Free Press, 2003), 64.

13. Moe-Lobeda, *Resisting Structural Evil*, 87.

14. Dwight N. Hopkins, *Down, Up, and Over: Slave Religion and Black Theology* (Minneapolis: Fortress Press, 2000), 228.

15. James H. Cone, *The Cross and the Lynching Tree* (Maryknoll, NY: Orbis, 2011), 31. Cone is quoting Paula Fredriksen, *Jesus of Nazareth, King of the Jews: A Jewish Life and the Emergence of Christianity* (New York: Vintage, 2000), 233–34.

16. Richard Perry, "Justification by Faith and Its Social Implications," in *Theology and the Black Experience: The Lutheran Heritage Interpreted by African and African-American Theologians*, ed. Albert Pero and Ambrose Moyo (Minneapolis: Fortress Press, 2009), 17–18.

17. Perry, "Justification by Faith and Its Social Implications," 18.

18. Cone, *Speaking the Truth*, 32. Cone goes on to quote Edward P. Wimberly and Anne Streaty Wimberly: "In black religious experience, justification cannot be correctly understood apart from black people's struggle for historical liberation. Liberation is not simply a consequence of the experience of sanctification. Rather,

sanctification is liberation. To be sanctified is to be liberated—that is, politically engaged in the struggle of freedom." Edward P. Wimberly and Anne Streaty Wimberly, *Liberation and Human Wholeness: The Conversion Experiences of Black People in Slavery and Freedom* (Nashville: Abingdon, 1986), 94–95.

19. Cynthia S. W. Crysdale, *Embracing Travail: Retrieving the Cross Today* (New York: Continuum, 2001), 25.

20. Cone, *The Cross and the Lynching Tree*, 18.

21. Dean Garrett Stroud, *Preaching in Hitler's Shadow: Sermons of Resistance in the Third Reich* (Grand Rapids: Eerdmans, 2013), 42.

22. Stroud, *Preaching in Hitler's Shadow*, 34. Stroud is referencing Max Lackmann, "Herr, wohin sollen wir gehen? Ein Wort eines Theologiestudenten an seine Kommilitonen" [Lord, Where Should We Go? A Word from a Theology Student to His Fellow Students], in *Theologishe Existenz Heute* [Theological Existence Today] (Munich: Ch. Kaiser, 1934), 4.

23. Dietrich Bonhoeffer, *Barcelona, Berlin, New York: 1928–1931*, ed. Clifford J. Green, trans. Douglas W. Stott, Dietrich Bonhoeffer Works 10 (Minneapolis: Augsburg Fortress, 2008), 288–89.

24. As quoted in "Martin Niemöller: 'First they came for the socialists. . .,'" *Holocaust Encyclopedia*, U.S. Holocaust Memorial Museum, https://tinyurl.com/yaj53q57.

25. Moe-Lobeda, *Resisting Structural Evil*, 75.

26. Stanley Hauerwas and Jean Vanier, *Living Gently in a Violent World: The Prophetic Witness of Weakness* (Downers Grove, IL: InterVarsity, 2008), 41.

27. Williams, *Bonhoeffer's Black Jesus*, 20.

28. Williams, *Bonhoeffer's Black Jesus*, 5.

29. Dietrich Bonhoeffer, "The Church and the Jewish Question," in *No Rusty Swords: Letters, Lectures and Notes, 1928–1936*, ed. Edwin H. Robertson, trans. Edwin H. Robertson and John Bowden, Collected Works of Dietrich Bonhoeffer 1 (New York: Harper, 1965), 225.

30. Craig L. Nessan, *Orthopraxis or Heresy: The North American Theological Response to Latin American Liberation Theology* (Atlanta: Scholars, 1989), 4.

31. Dietrich Bonhoeffer, *Letters and Papers from Prison*, 3rd ed., trans. Reginald H. Fuller (New York: Macmillan, 1967), 158.

32. Lyle D. Vander Broek, *Breaking Barriers: The Possibilities of Christian Community in a Lonely World* (Grand Rapids: Brazos, 2002), 24.

33. Moe-Lobeda, *Resisting Structural Evil*, 126. She is quoting Erich Fromm, *The Art of Loving* (New York: Harper, 1956), 125.

34. Nessan, *Orthopraxis or Heresy,* 107.

35. Yascha Mounk, "It's Time for an Outrage Armistice," *Slate*, May 2, 2018, https://tinyurl.com/yxp46vhu.

36. Anand Giridharadas, "What Woke America and Great America Can Learn from Each Other," *Huffington Post*, March 17, 2018, https://tinyurl.com/y6q53thr.

37. Hopkins, *Down, Up, and Over*, 230.

CHAPTER 5: HERE WE STAND

1. Craig Nessan, "Luther against the Jews: The Ethics of Historical Interpretation," *Currents in Theology and Mission* 45, no. 1 (January 2018), 5–10. Note also the fine work, referenced by Dr. Nessan, of Brooks Schramm and Kirsi I. Stjerna, eds., *Martin Luther, the Bible, and the Jewish People: A Reader* (Minneapolis: Fortress Press, 2012).

2. Alon Goshen-Gottstein, "Luther and the Jews—500 Years Later," The Blogs, *Times of Israel*, October 27, 2017, https://tinyurl.com /yyootpoz.

3. Phyllis Tickle, "The Great Emergence," *Radical Grace* (Center for Action and Contemplation) 21, no. 4 (2008): 4–5.

4. Paul Crutzen, "Geology of Mankind," *Nature* 514, no. 23 (2002): doi.org/10.1038/4150239.

5. Robinson Meyer, "The Grim Conclusions of the Largest-Ever Study of Fake News," *The Atlantic*, March 8, 2018, https://tinyurl.com/y6c28fhl.

6. "Nine Charts about Wealth Inequality in America (Updated)," Urban Institute, October 5, 2017, https://tinyurl.com/y37p9xra.

7. "Global Inequality," Inequality.org, Institute for Policy Studies, n.d., https://tinyurl.com/y3kudgp6.

8. Cynthia Hess et al., executive summary of *The Status of Women in the States: 2015*, Institute for Women's Policy Research, May 2015, https://tinyurl.com/y3fa2y3f.

9. CAP Immigration Team and Michael D. Nicholson, "The Facts on Immigration Today: 2017 Edition," Center for American Progress, April 20, 2017, http://tinyurl.com/yczunwsg; Leighton Ku and Brian Bruen, "Poor Immigrants Use Public Benefits at a Lower Rate than Poor Native-Born Citizens," CATO Institute, March 4, 2013, http://tinyurl.com/z5ov7nb.

10. Katayoun Kishi, "Assaults against Muslims in U.S. Surpass 2001 Level," Pew Research Center, November 15, 2017, http://tinyurl.com/y2e4hwby.

11. "2017 Audit of Anti-Semitic Incidents," Anti-Defamation League, http://tinyurl.com/y58ku729.

12. William H. Frey, "The US Will Become 'Minority White' in 2045, Census Projects," Brookings, March 14, 2018, http://tinyurl.com/y79ya3qr.

13. Janet Reitman, "U.S. Law Enforcement Failed to See the Threat of White Nationalism; Now They Don't Know How to Stop It," *New York Times Magazine*, November 3, 2018, http://tinyurl.com/ycd5d2lp.

14. Jonathan Haidt, "The Ethics of Globalism, Nationalism, and Patriotism," *Minding Nature* (Center for Humans and Nature) 9, no. 3 (Fall 2016), https://tinyurl.com/y5s7eb97.

15. Jack Jenkins, "Why Christian Nationalists Love Trump," *Think Progress*, August 7, 2017, https://tinyurl.com/yy2e7pwx.

16. Niraj Chokshi, "Trump Voters Driven by Fear of Losing Status, Not Economic Anxiety, Study Finds," *New York Times*, April 24, 2018, https://tinyurl.com/y2ujcvtm.

17. Jack Jenkins, "How Trump's Presidency Reveals the True Nature of Christian Nationalism," *Think Progress*, September 13, 2017, https://tinyurl.com/y3q4yo4j.

18. Rev. William Barber, leader of the Poor People's Campaign, who is often identified not just with the religious left, but as a leader of it, rejects the term out of hand. He has said, "There is no religious left and religious right. . . . There is only a moral center. And the scripture is very clear about where you have to be to be in the moral center—you have to be on the side of the poor, the working, the sick, the immigrant." Lauren Gambino, "'Jesus Never Charged a Leper a Co-pay': The Rise of the Religious Left," *Guardian*, May 21, 2018, https://tinyurl.com/y2h69td5.

19. Sarah Mervosh, "Nearly 40,000 People Died from Guns in U.S. Last Year, Highest in 50 Years," *New York Times*, December 18, 2018, http://tinyurl.com/y64pqdrc.

20. Dean Garrett Stroud, *Preaching in Hitler's Shadow: Sermons of Resistance in the Third Reich* (Grand Rapids: Eerdmans, 2013), 26. Quoting from Michael Burleigh, *The Third Reich: A New History* (New York: Hill & Wang, 2000), 252.

21. Dorothee Sölle, *Suffering*, trans. Everett R. Kalin (Minneapolis: Fortress Press, 1975), 36–37.

22. Bill Bishop, *The Big Sort: Why the Clustering of Like-Minded America Is Tearing Us Apart* (New York: Houghton Mifflin Harcourt, 2009).

CHAPTER 6: HERE WE IMAGINE

1. Krista Tippett, "Esther Sternberg: Stress and the Balance Within," interview with Esther Sternberg, *On Being*, last updated September 4, 2008, https://tinyurl.com/y3mwq9xl.

2. Darby Kathleen Ray, *Theology That Matters: Ecology, Economy, and God* (Minneapolis: Fortress Press, 2006), 159–61.

3. Walter Brueggemann, *Israel's Praise: Doxology against Idolatry and Ideology* (Philadelphia: Fortress Press, 1988), 12.

4. Walter Brueggemann, unpublished address at the Fund for Theological Education's Conference on Excellence in Ministry, housed

at Vanderbilt University, Summer 2001, as cited in Cynthia Moe-Lobeda's *Resisting Structural Evil: Love as Ecological-Economic Vocation* (Minneapolis: Fortress Press, 2013), 87.

5. Eugene Peterson, *Under the Unpredictable Plant: An Exploration in Vocational Holiness* (Grand Rapids: Eerdmans, 1994), 169–70.
6. James H. Cone, *Speaking the Truth: Ecumenism, Liberation, and Black Theology* (Maryknoll, NY: Orbis, 1999), 35.
7. Thomas Jefferson (1743–1826), "An Act for Establishing Religious Freedom, 16 January 1786," Manuscript, Records of the General Assembly, Enrolled Bills, Record Group 78, Library of Virginia, Richmond, Virginia, http://tinyurl.com/y6h548nz.
8. "Jefferson's Letter to the Danbury Baptists," January 1, 1802, Library of Congress, http://tinyurl.com/8uox6.
9. See 'Tax Guide for Churches & Religious Organizations," Department of the Treasury Interal Revenue Service, http://tinyurl.com /y3a3vl94. The ELCA has written an excellent guide for election activity, outlining what is and what is not permissible for tax-exempt institutions: "Being a Public Church," Evangelical Lutheran Church in America, http://tinyurl.com/y6s9gq7l. Note that any of this information is subject to change; before engaging in any activity, an attorney or local IRS official should be consulted.
10. Dwight N. Hopkins, *Down, Up, and Over: Slave Religion and Black Theology* (Minneapolis: Fortress Press, 2000), 252.
11. Cone, *Speaking the Truth*, 10. Søren Kierkegaard himself anticipated this very church when he described how he believed that the church ought to be lived out: "The conflict about Christianity will no longer be doctrinal conflict (this is the conflict between orthodoxy and heterodoxy). The conflict (occasioned also by the social and communistic movements) will be about Christianity as an existence. The problem will become one of loving the 'neighbor': attention will be directed to Christ's life, and Christianity will also become essentially accentuated in the direction of conformity to this life. The world has gradually consumed those masses of illusions and insulating walls with which we have protected ourselves so that the question remained simply one of Christianity as doctrine. The rebellion in the world shouts: We want to see action!"

Søren Kierkegaard's Journals and Papers, ed. and trans. Howard V. Hong and Edna H. Hong, vol. 4, *S–Z* (Bloomington: Indiana University Press, 1975), 172–73.

12. Walter Bouman, *Jesus Is Risen: Theology for the Church: The Lifework and Teaching of the Rev. Dr. Walter R. Bouman, Th.D*, vol. 2, ed. Ann M. Haut (Minneapolis: Lutheran University Press, 2015), 32–33.

13. See *Vision and Expectations: Ordained Ministers in the Evangelical Lutheran Church in America*, Evangelical Lutheran Church in America, Easter 2010, http://tinyurl.com/yycefdus. According to section IV, "Faithful Witness," ordained leaders are charged to engage in hospitality, peacemaking, justice speaking and seeking, and the stewardship of the earth (15–17).

BIBLIOGRAPHY

Baylor, Michael G. *The Radical Reformation*. Cambridge Texts in the History of Political Thought. Cambridge: Cambridge University Press, 1991.

Bishop, Bill. *The Big Sort: Why the Clustering of Like-Minded America Is Tearing Us Apart*. Boston: Mariner, 2008.

Bonhoeffer, Dietrich. *Discipleship*. Edited by Geffrey B. Kelly and John D. Godsey. Translated by Reinhard Krauss and Barbara Green. Dietrich Bonhoeffer Works 4. Minneapolis: Fortress Press, 2001.

———. *Letters and Papers from Prison*. 3rd ed. Translated by Reginald H. Fuller. London: SCM, 1967.

Bouman, Walter R., and Ann M. Haut. *Jesus Is Risen: Theology for the Church; the Lifework and Teaching of the Rev. Dr. Walter R. Bouman*. Minneapolis: Lutheran University Press, 2015.

Bouman, Walter R., Nancy M. Raabe, and Ann M. Haut. *Alleluia! A Gedenkschrift in Thanksgiving for the Life of Walter R. Bouman (1929–2005)*. Minneapolis: Lutheran UP, 2015.

Brueggemann, Walter. *Israel's Praise: Doxology against Idolatry and Ideology.* Philadelphia: Fortress Press, 1988.

Cannon, Katie Geneva. *Katie's Canon.* New York: Continuum, 2003.

Chokshi, Niraj. "Trump Voters Driven by Fear of Losing Status, Not Economic Anxiety, Study Finds." *New York Times*, April 24, 2018, https://tinyurl.com/y2ujcvtm.

Cobb, John B., Bruce Gordon Epperly, Paul S. Nancarrow, and Marjorie Suchocki. *The Call of the Spirit: Process Spirituality in a Relational World.* Claremont, CA: P & F, 2005.

Cone, James H. *The Cross and the Lynching Tree.* Grand Rapids: Eerdmans, 1986.

———. *Speaking the Truth: Ecumenism, Liberation, and Black Theology.* Grand Rapids: Eerdmans, 1999.

Crysdale, Cynthia S. W. *Embracing Travail: Retrieving the Cross Today.* New York: Continuum, 2001.

Fredriksen, Paula. *Jesus of Nazareth, King of the Jews: A Jewish Life and the Emergence of Christianity.* New York: Vintage, 2000.

George, Meta. *Recordings of Joseph Sittler: Summaries of Audio Recordings Held in the Sittler Archives.* Chicago: Joseph Sittler Archives, Lutheran School of Theology at Chicago, 2009.

Goldstein, Valerie Saiving. "The Human Situation: A Feminine View." *Journal of Religion* 40, no. 2 (1960): 100–12.

Greive, Wolfgang. *Justification in the World's Context.* Geneva: Lutheran World Federation, Office for Theology and the Church, 2000.

Hackett, Erna Kim. "Why I Stopped Talking about Racial Reconciliation and Started Talking about White Supremacy." *Feisty Thoughts* (blog), August 23, 2017, https://tinyurl.com/y3nkq7t5.

Haidt, Jonathan. "The Ethics of Globalism, Nationalism, and Patriotism." *Minding Nature* (Center for Humans and Nature) 9, no. 3 (Fall 2016), https://tinyurl.com/y5s7eb97.

Hauerwas, Stanley, and Jean Vanier. *Living Gently in a Violent World: The Prophetic Witness of Weakness.* Downers Grove, IL: InterVarsity, 2008.

Hess, Cynthia, et al. Executive summary of *The Status of Women in the States: 2015.* Institute for Women's Policy Research, May 2015, https://tinyurl.com/y3fa2y3f.

Hopkins, Dwight N. *Down, Up, and Over: Slave Religion and Black Theology.* Minneapolis: Fortress Press, 2000.

Hotchkiss, Sandy. *Why Is It Always about You? The Seven Deadly Sins of Narcissism.* New York: Free Press, 2003.

Institute for Policy Studies. "Global Inequality." Inequality.org, https://tinyurl.com/y3kudgp6.

Jenkins, Jack. "How Trump's Presidency Reveals the True Nature of Christian Nationalism." *Think Progress*, September 13, 2017, https://tinyurl.com/y3q4yo4j.

———. "Why Christian Nationalists Love Trump." *Think Progress*, August 7, 2017, https://tinyurl.com/yy2e7pwx.

Kierkegaard, Søren. *Søren Kierkegaard's Journals and Papers.* Edited and translated by Howard Vincent Hong and Edna Hatlestad Hong. 7 vols. Bloomington: Indiana University Press, 1975.

Lackmann, Max. "Herr, wohin sollen wir gehen? Ein Wort eines Theologiestudenten an seine Kommilitonen" [Lord, Where Should We Go? A Word from a Theology Student to His Fellow Students]. In *Theologische Existenz Heute* [Theological Existence Today]. Munich: Ch. Kaiser, 1934.

Luther, Martin. "The Large Catechism." In *The Book of Concord*, edited by Robert Kolb and Timothy J. Wengert. Minneapolis: Fortress Press, 2000.

Meyer, Robinson. "The Grim Conclusions of the Largest-Ever Study of Fake News." *The Atlantic,* March 8, 2018, https://tinyurl.com/y6c28fhl.

Moe-Lobeda, Cynthia D. *Healing a Broken World: Globalization and God.* Minneapolis: Fortress Press, 2002.

———. *Resisting Structural Evil: Love as Ecological-Economic Vocation.* Minneapolis: Fortress Press, 2013.

Mounk, Yascha. "It's Time for an Outrage Armistice." *Slate,* May 2, 2018, https://tinyurl.com/yxp46vhu.

Nessan, Craig L. *Orthopraxis or Heresy: The North American Theological Response to Latin American Liberation Theology.* Atlanta: Scholars, 1989.

Pero, Albert, and Ambrose Moyo, eds. *Theology and the Black Experience: The Lutheran Heritage Interpreted by African and African-American Theologians.* Minneapolis: Fortress Press, 2009.

Peterson, Eugene H. *Under the Unpredictable Plant: An Exploration in Vocational Holiness.* Grand Rapids: Eerdmans, 1994.

Powell, Mark Allan. "Salvation in Luke-Acts." In "Luke-Acts," special issue, *Word and World* 12, no. 1 (Winter 1992): 5–10.

Ray, Darby Kathleen. *Theology That Matters: Ecology, Economy, and God.* Minneapolis: Fortress Press, 2006.

Reitman, Janet. "U.S. Law Enforcement Failed to See the Threat of White Nationalism; Now They Don't Know How to Stop It." *New York Times Magazine*, November 3, 2018, https://tinyurl.com/y4xambnb.

Schramm, Brooks, and Kirsi I. Stjerna. *Martin Luther, the Bible, and the Jewish People: A Reader.* Minneapolis: Fortress Press, 2012.

Sölle, Dorothee. *Political Theology.* Translated by John Shelley. Philadelphia: Fortress Press, 1974.

———. *Suffering.* Translated by Everett Kalin. Philadelphia: Fortress Press, 1975.

Sternberg, Esther M. *The Balance Within: The Science Connecting Health and Emotions.* New York: W. H. Freeman, 2001.

Stroud, Dean Garrett. *Preaching in Hitler's Shadow: Sermons of Resistance in the Third Reich.* Grand Rapids: Eerdmans, 2013.

Tannehill, Robert C. "What Kind of King? What Kind of Kingdom? A Study of Luke." In "Luke-Acts," special issue, *Word and World* 12, no. 2 (Winter 1992).

Thompson, Deanna A. *Crossing the Divide: Luther, Feminism, and the Cross.* Minneapolis: Fortress Press, 2004.

Tickle, Phyllis. "The Great Emergence." *Radical Grace* (Center for Action and Contemplation) 21, no. 4 (2008): 4–5.

————. *The Great Emergence: How Christianity Is Changing and Why.* Grand Rapids: Baker, 2012.

Tippett, Krista. "Esther Sternberg: Stress and the Balance Within." Interview with Esther Sternberg. *On Being,* last updated September 4, 2008, https://tinyurl.com/y3mwq9xl.

Urban Institute. "Nine Charts about Wealth Inequality in America (Updated)." October 5, 2017, https://tinyurl.com /y37p9xra.

Vander Broek, Lyle D. *Breaking Barriers: The Possibilities of Christian Community in a Lonely World.* Grand Rapids: Brazos, 2002.

Williams, Reggie L. *Bonhoeffer's Black Jesus: Harlem Renaissance Theology and an Ethic of Resistance.* Waco, TX: Baylor University Press, 2014.

Wimberly, Edward P., and Anne Streaty Wimberly. *Liberation and Human Wholeness: The Conversion Experiences of Black People in Slavery and Freedom.* Nashville: Abingdon, 1986.

WORD & WORLD
BOOKS

THEOLOGY FOR CHRISTIAN MINISTRY

Informing and inspiring Christian leaders and communities to proclaim God's *Word* to a *World* God created and loves. Articulating the fullness of both realities and the creative intersection between them.

Word & World Books is a partnership between Luther Seminary, the board of the periodical *Word & World*, and Fortress Press.

Books in the series include:

Future Faith: Ten Challenges Reshaping Christianity in the 21st Century by Wesley Granberg Michaelson (2018)

Liberating Youth from Adolescence by Jeremy P. Myers (2018)

Elders Rising: The Promise and Peril of Aging by Roland Martinson (2018)

I Can Do No Other: The Church's New Here We Stand Moment by Anna M. Madsen (2019)

Intercultural Church: A Biblical Vision for an Age of Migration by Safwat Marzouk (2019)